EUROPA  MILITARIA I

CW00704896

British
24 AIRMOBILE BRIGADE

CARL SCHULZE

The Crowood Press

First published in 1999 by
The Crowood Press Ltd
Ramsbury, Marlborough
Wiltshire SN8 2HR

British Library Cataloguing-in-Publication Data
A catalogue record for this book is available from the British Library

ISBN 1 86126 276 0

Designed by Frank Ainscough/Compendium
Printed and bound by Craft Print Pte Ltd

Acknowledgements
During the research for this book I was assisted by so many officers, NCOs and men of 24 Airmobile Brigade that it is impossible to name them all; but I must extend special thanks to Major Ian Rigden, Major Tim Watts, Captain Ian Clooney, Squadron Leader Peter Martin, Captain Samantha Erskine Tulloch, Captain Doris Foxley, Captain Tim Marston, Captain McBride and Mr. Simon Smith. Thanks also to Mrs. Birgit Bröse Baumann and Mr. Mario Borchers. For official photographs I wish to thank the following companies and their public relations managers: Shorts Missile Systems Limited, GKN Westland, Racal Corporate Communications Centre, and Euromissile Dynamics Group. Special thanks also to Mr. Yves Debay who provided additional photographs; and to Ms. Britta Nurmann, without whose help and support this book would not have been possible.

Last but not least, I would like to apologize to the soldier of 1 RGBW to whom I explained that the pouring rain was "the best weather for infantry". I can understand that he did not appreciate this piece of information.

(Front cover photograph)
An infantryman of the 1st Royal Anglians, one of a "chalk" just landed by a Lynx Mk.9 LBH of 3 Regt., Army Air Corps. He wears the 24 Airmobile Brigade patch on his left sleeve; and carries one of his section's two 5.56mm Light Support Weapons. Basically an L85A1 (SA80) assault rifle with a longer, heavier barrel and a bipod, the LSW is used in the light machine gun role. At 970m/sec (3,182ft/sec) its muzzle velocity is 30m/sec (98ft/sec) higher than that of the basic rifle; it is also heavier, at 6.88kg (15lbs), and longer, at 900mm (35.4ins). The LSW and L85A1 otherwise have most parts in common and use the same 30-round magazines.

(Back cover photograph)
Two Chinook HC2 helicopters of the RAF Support Helicopter Force prepare to lift 105mm Light Guns of 28/143 (Tombs' Troop) Battery, 19 Regiment Royal Artillery to the next firing position. The crews, ammunition and equipment are already aboard.

Contents

Introduction

Airmobility can be summarized as the ability to move combat forces and their equipment across the battlefield by helicopters to engage in ground combat, avoiding the ground restrictions of the battlefield. The helicopter is used both as tactical transport for the ground forces and as an airmobile weapons platform to deliver fire support. In today's British armed forces order of battle, 24 Airmobile Brigade, with its headquarters at Colchester in Essex, is tasked with this role.

The brigade is a "square" formation of two infantry battalions, two aviation regiments, an artillery regiment with 24 x 105mm guns, an engineer field squadron, and all necessary combat service and support elements to allow it to operate nearly independently. Additional medium and heavy lift capacity is provided by an RAF Support Helicopter Force with Pumas and Chinooks. The manoeuvre units of the brigade are the two infantry battalions with the heavy anti-tank firepower of their 42 Milan ATGW systems; and the two Army Air Corps regiments each with 12 TOW-armed Lynx, 12 Gazelle and 11 Lynx Mk.9 light battlefield helicopters.

For airmobile operations each of these units provides assets to form one or more combined arms battle groups, which normally comprise infantry, aviation, artillery support, air defence, engineer and medical assets. With their tactical mobility the brigade and its battle groups are able to move around the battlefield by day or night with a high speed of execution, independent of ground obstacles, over a long range, and thus to catch the enemy by surprise.

For e.g. a division or corps commander, this means that he can field a reserve which can operate simultaneously with other formations, but without blocking advance routes to enter the battle. The brigade can operate at a higher speed than enemy ground forces; it is thus an ideal asset in a number of threatening situations, e.g. for flank attacks into enemy armoured thrusts which break through the front line. Once an operation is finished the airmobile force can easily be withdrawn, handing over to other units and restoring its resources so that it is ready to be committed again after a short time. The special capabilities of 24 Airmobile Brigade allow it –

To attack from any direction
To delay a larger force without becoming decisively engaged
To concentrate, disperse or redeploy rapidly
To provide responsive reserve and reaction forces
To react rapidly to tactical opportunities, placing forces at decisive points
To provide surveillance and target acquisition or screens over wide areas
To react to rear threats
To bypass enemy positions
To facilitate surprise and deception
To rapidly reinforce committed units.

Operations can include the channeling of enemy forces to pursue, block and counter penetration; deception and distraction, to cover larger formation attacks; operational security, including flank protection; raids on key targets, and the seizure of key terrain to allow exploitation, e.g. bridges that are needed for a larger formation attack; finding, delaying and containing enemy forces; and supporting the withdrawal of own forces.

Today's 24 Airmobile Brigade insignia, worn on the left shoulder, is the family crest of the late Lt Gen. Sir Frederick "Boy" Browning GCVO, KBE, CB, DSO, DL, who commanded 24 Guards Brigade in 1941, and later 1st Airborne Division and 1st Airborne Corps. It shows the wings of a gryphon in Army red on blue symbolising the sky.

Despite all the advantages enjoyed by an airmobile formation there are also some limitations: vulnerability to main armoured thrusts; the relative immobility of the infantry once it is deployed in the field, due to lack of ground transport; limited protection for the infantry; and night and weather restrictions. In addition to this the helicopters are easy targets for enemy attack aircraft and air defence artillery and, when flying at low level during operations, even for enemy small arms fire. The helicopter borne infantry are particularly vulnerable at the moment of deployment or extraction by air, and while they are digging in. Once they are on the ground enemy air strikes remain a threat due to the limited air defence capacity.

Even given these limitations, the tactical employment of the brigade can change the situation on the battlefield by massing or shifting combat power rapidly to take the enemy unawares. Surprise can be achieved or exploited; the initiative can be gained and maintained, by changing the speed of the battle and conducting simultaneous operations. 24 Airmobile Brigade can also extend the depth and breadth of the battlefield to allow own ground forces to operate more freely.

Build-up of operations

Immediately after the brigade is alerted and assigned to an operational theatre, advance recce elements will deploy, search for suitable locations, and link up with the allied HQ in the area. The advance recce parties consist of officers and men from all

Land Rover Defender 110 (in Army terms, Truck Utility Medium) and Defender 90 (Truck Utility Light) are the workhorses of the airmobile units, hardtops and softops being used in a variety of roles. This TUM "fitted for radio" (FFR) is stripped down for recce use by 1st Royal Gloucestershire, Berkshire and Wiltshire Regiment (1 RGBW). Powered by a 2.5 litre 4-cylinder diesel engine, it has a maximum weight of 3050kg (6,710lbs) and a top road speed of about 110km/h (68mph). Note the stowed equipment and LAW 80.

brigade units, so that all important factors can be taken into account. Parallel to this process the brigade elements back at Colchester will prepare vehicles and equipment for deployment.

Once preparations and reconnaissance are completed the brigade will deploy its elements to the Points of Embarkation; these can be airports like the Air Mounting Centre, or seaports, or a mixture of both. From here the units are flown and shipped to the Port/Airport of Deployment; and from there they are transferred to the Theatre Holding Area (THA), where flown-in personnel and shipped vehicles are linked up and further preparation for the operation is carried out. All movement is co-ordinated by the Movement Control Command Post.

From the THA the brigade will then deploy forward into a Brigade Staging Area, e.g. under command of the MND(C) – see page 60. In the BSA each unit has its own location where it carries out final preparations, including small training exercises. The last of the battle load of stores and supplies are taken over, and movement orders are given. This phase also includes the cross-attachment of companies to form all-arms battle groups. The staging area is far behind the Forward Line of Own Troops

(FLOT) and relatively safe from enemy operations; from here the brigade will deploy to a Forward Operation Base (FOB) once an objective is given. This move is spearheaded by recce parties followed by the unit's main body. The FOB is situated approximately 120km (75m) short of the brigade objective, since that is the operational range of the brigade. From the FOB the combat elements will then launch the operation.

Usually a Forward Armament & Refueling Point (FARP) will be inserted first, covered by the aviation infantry company and anti-tank helicopters. Once this area is secure reinforcements will be flown in including air defence assets and a battery of artillery to form a fire base. Now the main body of an aviation battle group can use this location to launch further missions on enemy locations. The FARP and fire base are resupplied on a regular schedule and, if the future operational plan of the brigade requires it, can be enlarged to form a new FOB by moving in the so-called "Step-up" HQ, light airmobile dressing station, and logistic elements.

Brigade history

The history of formations bearing the number 24 dates back to 12 November 1914, when 24 Infantry Brigade was first formed as part of the 8th Division. By the time of its de-activation on 20 March 1919 the brigade had seen action at Neuve Chapelle, Auber Ridge, Ypres and the Somme, and two VCs had been awarded to men of its constituent battalions.

On 13 February 1940 the number was revived with the formation of 24 Guards Brigade to take part in the Norwegian campaign. Later renamed 24 Guards Independent Brigade Group,

the formation saw action in the North African desert and Italy. In 1947 the title reverted to 24 Infantry Brigade. Returning to Great Britain in 1955, the brigade was deployed to Kenya for security operations against the Mau-Mau rising in 1958-64. During this period the brigade also deployed to Kuwait in June 1961 to defend that country against a threatened Iraqi invasion. Other "fire brigade" operations took brigade elements to Zanzibar and Swaziland, and in 1964 to Aden, a posting which included punishing operations in the desert mountains of Radfan.

In 1967 the brigade moved back to the UK, being headquartered in Plymouth as part of the United Kingdom Strategic Reserve under 3rd Division. From 1959 3rd Division, together with 38 Group RAF, was tasked to develop an airportable concept for the Reserve to deploy anywhere in the world. Both formations conducted a number of exercises and formed a Joint Task Force Headquarters. With British withdrawal from the Persian Gulf region, Malaysia and Singapore in 1968, resources were now focused on NATO's defence of Western Europe. The task of 3rd Division was to form United Kingdom Mobile Force to support NATO units on the Continent. Conducting operational tours to Northern Ireland in 1969, 1970 and 1972, 24 Infantry Brigade moved to Barnard Castle in 1971 and to Topcliff in 1973. In 1970 the formation adopted the title 24 Airportable Brigade.

The year 1975 saw a major restructuring of the British defence system, which led to a temporary disbandment of 24 Airportable Brigade, followed by its retitling as 5 Field Force under command of 2nd Armoured Division in Osnabrück, Germany. Its mission here was to protect supply and logistic

During "Certain Shield 91" the 1st Bn The Gloucestershire Regiment was one of the brigade's three infantry battalions. Its All Terrain Mobile Platforms had just returned from the Gulf, and some desert camo was left visible to break up the shape when they were repainted for Europe. This ATMP carries Milan and a pintle-mounted GPMG; these vehicles operated very effectively, screening the battalion's position by "shoot and scoot" missions. The high cross-country mobility of the 6x6 ATMP is based on the low-pressure tyres, the limited weight, and an approach angle of 57 degrees.

installations in BAOR rear areas against enemy special forces, airborne or airmobile operations. In 1983, once more as 24 Infantry Brigade, it returned to Catterick in the UK when 2nd Infantry Division returned home as BAOR was reduced to three Germany-based divisions.

Into the air

Although helicopters were first used by British forces on operations in Malaya in 1948, and since then in nearly every conflict involving British forces, it was not until 1983 that trials with an airmobile infantry formation began. This was inspired by the experience of the French, who first used helicopters in a wide range of operations in Algeria; and more obviously by the enormous American use of helicopters in Vietnam as assault transports and weapons platforms. For the British trials 6 Brigade, under command of 3rd Division in Germany, was restructured into 6 Airmobile Brigade, ready in January 1984 and consisting of two infantry battalions (1st Gordon Highlanders and 1st, later 2nd Bn, Light Infantry), a field regiment RA, a field

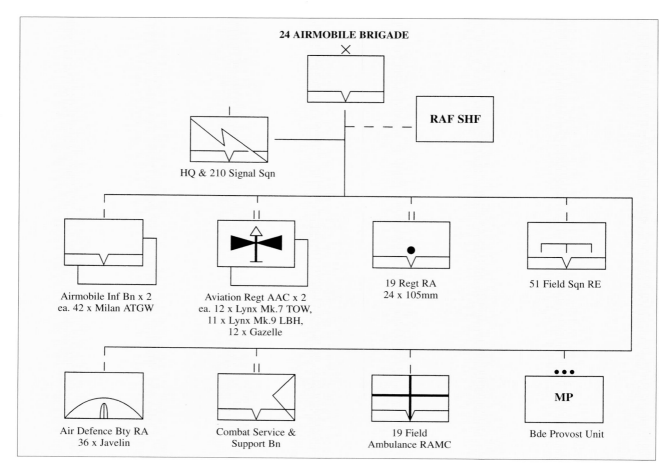

24 AIRMOBILE BRIGADE

RAF SHF

HQ & 210 Signal Sqn

Airmobile Inf Bn x 2
ea. 42 x Milan ATGW

Aviation Regt AAC x 2
ea. 12 x Lynx Mk.7 TOW,
11 x Lynx Mk.9 LBH,
12 x Gazelle

19 Regt RA
24 x 105mm

51 Field Sqn RE

Air Defence Bty RA
36 x Javelin

Combat Service &
Support Bn

19 Field
Ambulance RAMC

MP

Bde Provost Unit

squadron Royal Engineers, and an Army Air Corps squadron of Lynx anti-tank helicopters and Gazelle reconnaissance, liaison and general purpose light helicopters. To airlift its units the brigade had to rely on RAF transport helicopters.

The first positive results were achieved during the large exercise "Lion Heart 84", when the brigade was used both as a blocking force and as a deep penetration spearhead, seizing key objectives along the route of an armoured counter-attack. This success led to an extension of the trials until 1986, when 24 Brigade was permanently assigned to the new British airmobile force and 6 Airmobile Brigade was reformed as an armoured brigade. Officially 24 Airmobile Brigade adopted the airmobile role from 1988; the first brigade exercise was successfully carried out in 1989 under the name "Key Flight 89". The brigade was at first designed to be a defensive anti-tank heavy reserve blocking force, which could deploy rapidly to any point on the battlefield to channel and destroy advancing enemy armour breaking through the NATO forward defence line. It fielded three infantry battalions (1st Bn The Green Howards, 1st Bn The Duke of Edinburgh's Royal Regiment, and 1st Bn The Gloucestershire Regiment), as well as 9 Regiment Army Air Corps and brigade combat and service support units.

After the collapse of the Iron Curtain in the early 1990s, and the consequent change in NATO strategy to the rapid reaction concept, 24 Airmobile Brigade changed its structure, losing one infantry battalion but receiving a second AAC regiment. The defensive airmobile anti-armour reserve role changed; the

brigade was now prepared for a wide range of missions including defensive and offensive operations in a variety of scenarios, under national or international command. In 1993 the brigade moved from Catterick to its current base at Colchester, and was assigned to NATO's newly formed Multinational Division Central (Airmobile), which was fully activated in 1994.

Although many brigade units have since been deployed on operations e.g. the Gulf War in 1991, or on rotation to Northern Ireland for internal security duties, 1995 saw the first operational deployment of the brigade itself. In July first advance elements of 24 Airmobile Brigade deployed to Bosnia while the main body carried out intensive training on Salisbury Plain to operate under United Nations command; this training included, e.g., negotiation skills and checkpoint procedures as well as live firing exercises and FIBUA training (Fighting in Built-Up Areas).

While 1st Bn The Light Infantry and 4th Regiment AAC remained in the UK as reserve, the rest of the brigade deployed to Ploce on the Croatian coast at the beginning of August 1995 to form part of the UN's Rapid Reaction Force for "Operation Hamden". By that date 19 Regiment Royal Artillery had already formed part of "Task Force Alpha" since the end of June, and was deployed along with French Foreign Legion units to Mount Igman above Sarajevo from 23 July to counter Serbian attacks on the Bosnian capital (see EuropaMilitaria No.22). 19/5 Battery RA was attached from the British AMF(L) contingent (see EM No.26), and replaced 19 Regt RA to provide artillery support for 24 Airmobile Brigade. While based on Mount Igman, 25/170

(Right) Insignia of brigade units at time of writing **(top to bottom, left to right):**
Sleeve patch, 210 Signal Sqn; sleeve patch, 24 Airmobile Bde; sleeve patch, 1st Royal Scots.
Cap badge, 1st Royal Scots; cap badge, B Coy 1 RS, Gurkha coy – note reversed tartan patch; cap badge, 1 RGBW with "Brandywine" flash.
Cap badge, Royal Engineers; cap badge, Army Air Corps, with shoulder slide of 4 Regt – red for 654 Sqn (Maiden of Warsaw), Lincoln green for 669 Sqn.; cap badge, Royal Artillery.
Cap badges, Royal Corps of Signals; Royal Logistic Corps; Royal Military Police; Royal Electrical & Mechanical Engineers; Royal Army Medical Corps.

(Left) Known in the brigade as the Ground Mobile Weapon Platform (GMWP), the Longline Light Strike Vehicle (LSV) is based on a high tensile tubular steel space frame. A VAG 1.9 turbo diesel engine gives a top speed of 130km/h (60mph) with a range of 200km (125 miles). Fully loaded the vehicle weighs 1.8 tons, making it a practical underslung load for both Puma and Chinook helicopters. Originally designed for operations demanding a stealthy approach and rapid exit, and used by the SAS in the Gulf, the LSV was first trialed for airmobile use during "Certain Shield 91" by 1st Bn The Green Howards. The LSV has a crew of two and can be used as a recce vehicle and mobile weapon platform, as here for a Milan.

7

(**Left**) Trigat MR will soon replace Milan as the British infantry ATGW system. With an operational range of between 200 and 2,400 yards against static and moving targets, its tandem warhead can penetrate explosive reactive armour, and adds the tactical ability to fire out of buildings. The firing post weighs 17kg (30lbs), as does a missile in its transport container. A thermal imaging sight can be mounted, weighing an additional 9.35kg. The laser guided missile takes 12 seconds to reach a target 2,000 yards away, which means that a well-trained crew can destroy three targets in one minute. (Photo courtesy Euromissile Dynamics Group).

(Imjin) and 28/143 (Tombs' Troop) Batteries of 19 Regiment each fired more than 500 rounds on enemy targets around Sarajevo, and the FDC of the regiment together with the FOO parties directed and co-ordinated all indirect fire in the region, including French artillery and Dutch mortars as well as air strikes. On several occasions the units were fired upon by the Serbs with small arms, mortars and artillery. At last "Operation Deliberate" led to the establishment at least for a time of peace in Bosnia. After a lot of operational work for the artillery and engineers and a long preparation for combat, the brigade units redeployed back to Britain in October 1995 just before the Dayton peace agreement was signed, although 24 Airmobile remained assigned to UNPROFOR as a rapid reaction asset up to the transfer of authority to IFOR in December 1995.

The operation in Bosnia demonstrated that the brigade, with its light equipment and wheeled support vehicles, can deploy rapidly to any theatre of operations. This strategic mobility depends on ships and transport aircraft to support the deployment, however. In the case of "Operation Hamden" this was partially carried out by Startlifters of the USAF Air Mobility Command, which flew over 110 missions and moved more than 2,000 personnel and 1,700 tons of cargo. The rest of the deployment was flown in by RAF aircraft; most of the vehicles were ferried to Ploce by hired merchant ships.

The future: new weapons, new role

In summer 1995 the Ministry of Defence placed an order for 67 McDonnel Douglas Apache AH64D Longbow attack helicopters, to be assembled by GKN Westland under licence. It is assumed that the helicopters will be divided between the AAC regiments of 24 Airmobile Brigade and 3rd Division, a third batch being used for training, trials and as War Maintenance Reserve (WMR). The Apache, which will replace the AAC Lynx Mk.7 anti-tank helicopters in approximately 2000, will bring fundamental changes in the brigade's tactics. By the time of writing the brigade was carrying out trials to fit the new capabilities of the Apache AH64D into the brigade's Standing Operational Procedures by the time of delivery.

In the past the Lynx anti-tank helicopter was mainly used defensively against attacking enemy armour and in support of ground troops; but the Apache Longbow allows an offensive role. With its rotor mast-mounted Longbow radar and target acquisition & designation sight it is possible to observe a 360 degree field. More than 1,000 targets can be recognized and classified, and 256 of them are shown to the pilot with their respective urgencies. In the ideal case the crew can now destroy 16 of these targets with their Hellfire rockets and attack others with the 30mm M230 chain gun. For self-defence four Stinger missiles can be mounted to the Apache Longbow.

The trials carried out by 24 Airmobile Brigade envisage the formation of an attack helicopter battle group which can carry out operations deep inside enemy territory. This means changes to the brigade's tactics, and the establishment of a structure capable of fighting an all-arms battle with the Apache Longbow as one of its key elements. Now the ground elements will support the helicopters in an "air-mechanized battle"; and the increased proportion of armed to transport helicopters even allows operations in which armed aviation forces conduct independent combat for a limited period without combat support by ground forces.

The Apache/Hellfire combination is not the only element in the brigade's enhanced antitank capabilities, which will be second to none. Milan will soon reach the end of its service, and the new ATGW system Trigat MR will take over its role. With Trigat MR enemy armour can be destroyed at ranges of between 200 and 2,400m, including all currently known types of armour.

On the vehicle side, at the time of writing the brigade is being issued the new Land Rover XD Wolf, and is awaiting the Ground Mobile Weapons Platform (GMWP); this modified Land Rover, from which heavy infantry weapons can be fired, will take the place of the Light Strike Vehicle (LSV) formerly used by the brigade.

The helicopter lift capacity of the SHF is also due to expand with the delivery of the first EH101 transports; operability of the first RAF squadron is planned by 2000.

Although 24 Airmobile Brigade and the airmobile concept are the youngest developments in the British order of battle, the changing political situation in Europe and unrest and instability in the Middle East and Africa show the need for a light, highly mobile force which can deal with a wide range of scenarios from peace keeping and peace enforcement to fighting a conventional war. The growing involvement of NATO forces in low intensity conflicts like the communal wars in the former Yugoslavia is an indicator of the type of operations the British Army will encounter in the future.

Today 24 Airmobile Brigade forms an important part of the MND(C), which comes under command of the Allied Rapid Reaction Corps. Simultaneously, elements of the brigade are permanently earmarked for Britain's Joint Rapid Deployment Force, which can support specifically British interests worldwide. The importance of the brigade will increase with the delivery of the new equipment; and it is only a question of time until the next operation which will involve the brigade's well-trained personnel. The 1998 Strategic Defence Review, which announced the latest restructuring of the British Army, also bears directly on 24 Airmobile Brigade.

For the future it is planned to replace the two airmobile infantry battalions of the brigade by airborne infantry battalions of the Parachute Regiment, the present 5 Airborne Brigade being re-roled as a mechanized formation. This will give 24 Airmobile Brigade the capability to insert advance forces into a theatre by use of a Leading Parachute Battalion Group (LPBG). Under this plan 24 Airmobile Brigade will be the Army's first and only air manoeuvre brigade, and thus the spearhead of Britain's JRRF. In the future 24 Airmobile Brigade will consist of three attack helicopter regiments and two airborne infantry battalions, together with artillery, engineer and other combat support and service assets. For the JRRF – which will also embrace 3 Commando Brigade (Royal Marines), and the "Ready Brigade" of 3rd (UK) Mechanized Division – it will provide the most readily available force for an immediate response. The brigade will participate in the lead parachute/tactical air landing operations battle group, and in the lead aviation/armoured reconnaissance battle group. Full implementation of the changes announced under the 1998 Strategic Defence Review is expected to be completed in 2001, in which year the JRRF will become operational.

(Below) The fearsome front view of the Apache AH64D Longbow. The frame is protected by lightweight boron carbide armour capable of stopping 12.7mm (.50cal) AP incendiary rounds. This photo shows eight Hellfire AT missiles, two 19-round pods of 70mm (2.75in) unguided rockets, and a 30mm M230 chain gun with 1,200 rounds. With its mast-mounted surveillance and target acquisition equipment, the Apache is a revolution in air/ground warfare. For defence against enemy aircraft it can also carry Stinger or Sidewinder AIM 9L missiles. With a two-man crew combat weight is 7480kg (16,456lbs); the Longbow version's Rolls Royce Turbomeca RTM 322 gives a speed of 265km/h (124mph). (Photo courtesy GKN Westland Helicopters)

The Airmobile Infantry Battalion

The main ground combat elements of 24 Airmobile Brigade are two airmobile infantry battalions with a heavy scale of anti-tank armament. British infantry battalions rotate through different assignments (the armoured role, light role, mechanized role, etc.) at least every four years; at the time of writing the airmobile units are 1st Bn The Royal Scots (The Royal Regiment), and 1st Bn The Royal Gloustershire, Berkshire and Wiltshire Regiment. The battalions are equally structured, and consist of three rifle companies (of which one is designated as the "aviation company"), a fire support company (also sometimes known as "recce company"), and an HQ and support company. All airmobile rifle companies are equally structured, except that the battalion aviation company fields eight Milan firing posts while the other two have ten. Further details about the company are given in the next chapter.

The six officers and 120 men of the fire support/recce company are organised into an HQ element, a mobile anti-tank platoon, a mortar platoon and a reconnaissance platoon. (With the anticipated reintroduction of the Browning M2 .50cal machine gun, it is believed that a fire support platoon will also be formed within the fire support/recce company; and that all infantry companies will be equipped with a mix of .50 MG and Milan, as will the recce platoon.) By drawing together the GPMGs of the battalion, it is also currently possible to form a temporary machine gun platoon if required. Usually this will field nine GPMGs in the sustained fire role, and can either be attached to the fire support/recce company or to one of the rifle companies.

Whereas an armoured infantry battalion of the British Army is normally equipped with 20 Milan firing posts, the airmobile infantry battalion fields 42 Milan systems. Ten of them are used by the mobile anti-tank platoon. This consists of five Milan detachments, each with two firing posts and an HQ detachment, the platoon totalling one officer and 34 other ranks. In the past the detachments were equipped with two Long Line LSVs each; at the time of writing these are due to be replaced with specially modified Land Rovers (the Army calls both vehicles Ground Mobile Weapon Platforms – GMWPs).

The reconnaissance platoon of one officer and 23 men is divided into three sections each equipped with two Land Rover 110 FFRs and two GMWPs. The platoon can mount four Milan ATGW systems and four GPMGs on their vehicles. When required the recce platoon and mobile anti-tank platoon can form a reconnaissance screen in front of the battalion, or work in the fighting withdrawal to slow down advancing enemy forces.

The mortar platoon of one officer and 56 ORs comprises nine 81mm L16A1 tubes which are divided between three sections of three. Each mortar and its four-man crew are transported in a Steyr-Pinzgauer with trailer; a Land Rover with the three-strong fire control party completes the 15-man section. Two Land Rovers FFR accomodate the platoon HQ. During operations the platoon can operate together to support the defensive battle of the battalion, or can be split up into sections and attached to the rifle companies or fire support/recce

The steady reduction of the British infantry by unit amalgamations has sometimes resulted in a rich mix of insignia, as new single units defend traditions recalling battle honours won by several predecessors over 350 years. The 1st Battalion, The Royal Gloucestershire, Berkshire and Wiltshire Regiment, amalgamated in 1994, is a prime example. 1 RGBW's immediate ancestors were The Gloucestershire Regiment, once the 28th Foot; and The Duke of Edinburgh's Royal Regiment (Berkshire & Wiltshire), once the 49th and 62nd Foot. Their dark blue general service beret bears the cross patée of the old 62nd or Wiltshires, charged with the Egyptian sphinx of the Glosters, all on the red "Brandywine" flash recalling the 49th or Berkshires' victory at that American Revolutionary action in 1777. (Beaten by the 49th's light company in a daring night attack, the Americans swore revenge – whereupon the British dyed their green hat tufts red so that the enemy could be sure of recognizing them in future). Uniquely, there is also a small "back badge" on the beret; like the sphinx, this recalls the 28th's valour at Alexandria in 1801, when the ranks fought back to back against heavy French attacks from two directions.

company; during raids or attacks on key targets the mortars can be deployed as part of the infantry companies' fire support groups. To enable the mortar teams to accomplish their fire missions fast and easily the platoon uses Morzon, a hand-held fire control computer system enabling them to calculate all necessary data. To transport mortars or additional ammunition in rough terrain the platoon also has five ATMPs.

All administrative and support work for the battalion is done by HQ company. In the nerve centre of the battalion, which on operations is built out of four Land Rover FFRs and some small tents, the battalion commander plans and leads the deployment and operations of his unit. In this he is supported by his HQ platoon and intelligence section, and the battalion's own signal platoon provides all necessary communications. The battalion HQ can be deployed forward during airmobile operations, so that the commander has close access to the

(Left) After getting the thumbs up signal from the co-pilot, men of 1 RGBW move to board a Puma HC1, approaching from the front so that they can be seen by the crew. They are equipped with personal weapons, webbing and "day packs" only. Pre-flight procedures for airmobile infantry include dividing the troops into "chalks" (in paratroop terms, sticks) each with a chalk commander. Equipment is prepared so that nothing can be blown away by the rotor wash. Any headgear other than helmets has to be taken off; radio antennae are dismounted and stowed; and troops are familiarized with the signals they might encounter.

During the flight weapons have to point downwards; they may be loaded but must be made safe.

(Below) A staff sergeant of 1 RGBW prepares an orange marking card before he uses it to guide a helicopter to his chalk. Once the chalk is on board the card is handed over to the crew; it bears the drop point grid reference, follow-on load with grid of pick-up point, and information on the current load, number of personnel, additional underslung loads, etc.

running battle. The heavier logistical part of the company, known as the "echelon", stays behind at the FOB. It comprises the quartermaster platoon, catering platoon, motor transport platoon, a REME section, a provost section and the regimental admin office. A light echelon termed AI can be flown forward on operations; this consists of a Land Rover FFR with the AI echelon commander, a small REME repair team, the RMO and a light RAP, and any ground dumped stores. During operations the battalion's medical section will run the battalion's first aid post and attach medics to each company. Altogether the HQ company consists of 11 officers and 159 NCOs and men.

In total the airmobile infantry battalion is 680 strong, with 38 officers and 642 other ranks. It fields 63 Land Rovers, 19 x 4-ton trucks, 23 x 8-ton trucks, 14 Trucks Utility Medium (Heavy Duty), 30 GMWPs, 13 ATMPs, 2 JCBs, 2 UBREs and 114 trailers.

(**Opposite, top**) Using the so called "golf bag" principle, a machine gun section formed by soldiers of the 1st Royal Scots awaits a lift by Puma helicopter. Once they are dropped they will act as a fire support group for an infantry attack. Mounting the GPMG on its tripod in the sustained fire format increases the weapon's effective range to 1800m with the C2 optical sight.

(**Left**) A lance-corporal operates a GPMG mounted on the roll bar of a Land Rover 110 FFR of Recce Platoon, 1st Royal Anglians. Note his subdued rank chevron worn on the sleeve below the yellow/red battle flash (recalling the old Suffolk Regiment, and the yellow and red roses picked by the 12th Foot as they went into battle at Minden in 1759). The belt-fed 7.62mm GPMG has a theoretical rate of fire of up to 750rpm. Dismounted on its bipod the useful range is 800m. With 50 rounds loaded the gun weighs13.85kg (30.47lbs).

(**Above**) Chalks for a lift by Chinook HC2 make their way to their pick-up point inside a helicopter landing site (HLS); the Chinook can carry at least 36 fully equipped infantrymen. In the foreground a section of the 1 RS mortar platoon have the three man-loads (base plate, barrel, and bipod with sight) strapped to the new type of camouflaged PLCE bergen rucksacks. These components of the 81mm L16A1 mortar weigh respectively 11.6kg (25.5lbs), 12.7kg (28lbs) and 13.55kg (29.8lbs).

(**Right**) One of the battalion's nine 81mm tubes; it has an effective range of 5.56km (3.4 miles). Rounds available include high explosive, smoke and illumination. Using a seven charge propellant system, all rounds have a weight of 4.2kg (9.24lbs) each. Here, during exercise "Gryphon's Eye 94" in Cophill Down on Salisbury Plain, a practice round is loaded by soldiers of the 1st Royal Anglians – the unit which handed over the airmobile role to the 1st Royal Scots.

(Left) Milan ATGW systems can be fired from the top of the LSV. Note the unit-improvised mounting on the vehicle's roll cage.

(Below) A crew from 1st Royal Anglians prepare their Milan ATGW firing post – here equipped with MIRA night sights – to engage armour. Milan can destroy enemy armour out to a range of 2000m; the Semi-Automatic Command to Line Of Sight (SACLOS) guidance system gives a hit guarantee of 98 per cent at that distance, and the operator only has to keep the aiming mark of the sight on the target. The firing post weighs 16.4kg (36lbs) and a missile with container 12.23kg (27lbs).

(Opposite, top left) Well camouflaged Milan-armed Supercat Mk.2 of the 1st Bn, The Green Howards, one of the three original infantry battalions of 24 Airmobile Bde. during exercise "Certain Shield 91". (When not tactical this battalion's vehicles fly green pennants with a white XIX, recalling their ancestors of the old 19th Foot.)

(Opposite, top right) Protected by a *shemagh* and Scott wind and dust goggles – two additions to kit which have proved very popular since the Gulf War – this driver of a recce Land Rover from 1 RGBW awaits orders to drive his vehicle up the rear ramp of a Chinook HC2. Note the Union flag patch, and privately acquired DPM chest webbing.

(Opposite, bottom) A Supercat Mk.2 of an airmobile infantry battalion is prepared for lifting by an RAF Chinook HC2 which has touched down nearby to pick up troops. Supercat Mk.2 can be carried as an internal load or underslung; a Chinook can hook on up to three of these 1650kg (3,630lb) runabouts. The 6x6 Supercat is powered by a VW 1900 4-cylinder diesel and has a road speed of up to 64km/h (40mph).

(Left) Most of his platoon's advance to the attack was covered by smoke; now this soldier of 1 RGBW closes in on the enemy position, suppressing resistance with roughly aimed fully automatic fire from his L85A1 rifle. When he is close enough to the enemy trench he will hurl in a grenade.

(Below) The airmobile infantry battalion HQ is situated inside four Land Rovers and is fully airportable. Here tents are attached to the rear of the vehicles to provide working space. The battalion HQ is the nerve centre of the infantry battle group, gathering and collating all information affecting the battalion commander's decisions for the current battle and future moves, incorporating the advice of his supporting staff from other arms of service.

Inside an Airmobile Infantry Company

In its structure and equipment B Company, 1st Battalion, The Royal Scots (The Royal Regiment) is a typical airmobile infantry company, similar in all essentials to the others of the brigade. What sets it apart is visible at first glance: far from being remotely Scottish, its soldiers are Gurkhas.

The 1st Royal Scots are one of those battalions which are currently unable to recruit up to the required strength from their traditional hunting grounds; and this solution was chosen, given the recent reduction of Gurkha infantry to just two battalions of The Royal Gurkha Rifles. With the disbandment of the Brigade of Gurkhas and the handover of Hong Kong – a longtime Gurkha posting – the Army stood to lose the services of many of these well trained and highly motivated Nepalese volunteers, the latest heirs to a fighting tradition in British service stretching back to 1815. (Other Gurkha companies are B Coy, 1st Bn, The Princess of Wales's Royal Regiment; and C Coy, 2nd Bn, The Parachute Regiment – both currently under 5 Airborne Brigade.) It is anticipated that home recruiting for the 1st Royal Scots will allow the Gurkhas' replacement in the year 2000. In the meantime these excellent soldiers are cementing a hundred-year-old tradition of battlefield comradeship between Scottish and Gurkha infantry.

Formed in November 1996, B Coy 1 RS underwent three weeks' formation training before it went over to the airmobile role; most of the 105 soldiers of the company were drawn from 1 RGR during the disbandment of 3 RGR and the reshuffling of Gurkha personnel. The following year saw the Gurkhas very busy, on exercises in Kenya, Germany and Canada as well as the UK, and providing "enemy forces" for other large exercises. They also earned the distinction of being named best British team in the 1997 Nijmegen long range marching competition. Today Gurkha recruits for 1 RGR come mainly from Western Nepal and 2 RGR recruits from Eastern Nepal. The basic training of a Gurkha infantryman takes ten months rather than the British infantry's normal six months. In addition to all the necessary military skills the training also includes English language lessons and an introductory course on the British way of life. The approximately 150 recruits of the Gurkha Recruit Company, part of the Gurkha Training Wing based at Church Crookham, normally reach a high standard of personal skills. Of the 1997 Course, 58 per cent finished their training as Rifle Marksmen, and this is not considered at all an outstanding figure.

Organised like any other airmobile infantry company, B Coy 1 RS consists of three rifle platoons and an HQ and support element. The *HQ and support element* consists of the TAC group, the HQ section and the echelon element. Each of the three *rifle platoons* is divided into three eight-man sections and a four strong platoon command section. The platoon commanders are Gurkha officers or senior NCOs, and the section commanders usually hold the rank of corporal. The eight men of the section are equipped with six Individual Weapons SA80 calibre 5.56mm (otherwise known as the L85A1 rifle), and two LSWs – the light

Soldier of B Coy, 1 RS, wearing the dark Rifle-green beret of his parent Royal Gurkha Rifles, with its crowned crossed kukris badge set on a flash of Hunting Stewart tartan marking attachment to the Royal Scots. While highly trained in the use of the most sophisticated modern weapons the Gurkhas still carry their traditional heavy-bladed kukri knife; they have a well-founded reputation for pressing home infantry assaults with fury, and the kukri is a practical, not to say a fearsome weapon in close quarter fighting.

support version of the weapon. In addition the platoon has a 51mm mortar and a 7.62mm GPMG which can be used either in the light role or, with a tripod, in the sustained fire role.

For communication the section commanders are equipped with PRC 349 radios, platoons being linked up to Coy HQ by PRC 350. Other radios used by the company are a mixture of PRC 351, PRC 352 and PRC 320 manpacks and VRC 353 vehicle radios. Since much of the movement is carried out by air the transport capabilities of the company's vehicles are limited. The company has two Land Rover FFR, one each for the OC and his 2iC; each platoon has one 4-ton truck and one Land Rover GS. In addition there are one Pinzgauer, two motorcycles and another 4-ton truck for the CQMS (Company Quartermaster Section). If required, the company can draw an ATMP from the battalion pool for cross-country load carrying.

In the battalion's aviation company eight Milan antitank guided weapon systems are gathered in one of the three platoons; the other two companies each field ten Milans. As many LAW 80 light anti-tank weapons as needed can be issued. For soft-skinned vehicles or the support weapon role the future will see the re-issue of the classic .50cal Browning M2 machine gun. For close-quarter battle each soldier is trained in the use of hand grenades and smoke grenades as well as illumination

(Left) As red smoke drifts away a Gurkha section or platoon leader (identified by his PRC 319 radio) prepares for a counter – attack during a FIBUA battle. He is armed with an L85A1 assault rifle fitted with the blank-firing attachment (painted yellow) which is used during exercises to produce enough gas pressure to recycle the action. Note the Mk.6 ballistic helmet worn without a cover, a common method of identifying one of the two sides during an exercise. His shoulder flash is the Hunting Stewart tartan identifying the Royal Scots – the old 1st Foot, the senior regiment of the Line, which traces its origins to a regiment raised by John Hepburn in 1633 with Royal sanction to serve the French King Louis XIII. It has since gained 147 battle honours during outstanding service to the British crown all over the world.

(Below) On the L85A1 of the foreground soldier is fitted a Common Weapon Sight, a third generation light intensifying device allowing targets up to 300m away to be engaged at night. The background soldier uses night vision goggles, which can be worn with a frame or, as here, like binoculars.

(Opposite, top right) This Gurkha sniper had to take off some of his camouflage to be visible to the camera. The weapon is the standard British L96A1 in 7.62mm, a bolt action rifle made by Accuracy; with a Schmidt & Bender 6x42 telescopic sight good snipers can engage targets out to 1200m. Within 24 Airmobile these highly skilled soldiers often form part of the recce elements.

(Opposite, bottom) For its own indirect fire support each infantry platoon has a 51mm light mortar weighing 6.275kg (13.8lbs), which can be carried and fired by one soldier. This can be used to fire smoke, illumination and HE rounds out to 750m; with a short range device it can be used in close-quarter battle with great accuracy.

pyrotechnics. For special tasks soldiers from all platoons can be drawn together to form an assault pioneer section or a reconnaissance section. Another special skill is provided by the company's two sniper teams, each consisting of a pair of soldiers – one sniper with the L96A1 rifle and one spotter armed with an LSW for close protection. On the modern battlefield most of the fighting happens at night; four Common Weapon Sights (CWS) and two pairs of night vision goggles are issued to each section. All the Milan systems can be fitted with MIRA (Milan InfraRed Attachment) to give night-fighting capability.

While all units of the British Army have their own Qualified Helicopter Handling Instructors, 24 Airmobile units undergo Airmobile Conversion Training at Wattisham airfield, which takes two weeks and is carried out by the unit's QHHI and instructors from the Army Air Corps and the RAF Support Helicopter Force. The goal of this training is to prepare each individual soldier for working with aircraft and to make them familiar with Lynx, Puma and Chinook helicopters. Lessons and practical training include how to recce and mark helicopter landing sites; enplaning and deplaning drills; equipment storage inside the helicopter; emergency drills and safety procedures for all types of helicopters used by British forces; preparing and despatching underslung and internal loads; guiding helicopters on the HLS; abseiling and fast roping from helicopters, as well as low level flights.

On operations or in battle the company can either work as part of the infantry battalion battle group or as an *aviation company*, which comes under command of one of the brigade's two AAC regiments. Their mission when attached to the AAC includes all regular infantry tasks, but also to provide defence for the aviation

assets of the aviation battle group, and to act as ground reconnaissance element for the helicopters in battle. Their range of tasks includes positional and mobile defence; offensive operations – attacks, reconnaissance patrols, ambushes, raids; and transitional operations – withdrawal, relief in place, relief in combat, advance to contact, rearward and forward passage of lines, etc.

The company works on the so-called "golf-bag principle": just as the golfer has a special club for every problem, so the commander can adapt the structure of the company according to the mission. Most of the company's heavy weapons are held by the CQMS; on the OC's orders a platoon will collect the .50 MGs and Milan launchers and act as a support platoon.

*　　*　　*

An attack on an enemy objective, e.g. an anti-aircraft defence position, bridge, artillery or rocket position, is spearheaded by recce elements of the attacking force deployed up to 72 hours in advance. They are usually flown in by helicopter but land far from the objective and march to it on foot so as to avoid detection. The recce troops establish observation posts and conduct patrols, passing as much information as possible back to the battle group commander planning the operation. The attacking force then also deploys by helicopter to an HLS far enough from the objective to be out of sight and hearing of the enemy. Here they link up with parts of the recce element, who guide the main body – split into attack, reserve and fire support forces – to their lines of departure.

Now the last part of the "find, fix and strike" operation unfolds. While the fire support group pin the enemy down in their trenches with Milans and machine guns, the attack group

closes in to engage. Additional (or even the only) fire support may be given by artillery deployed to a nearby fire base. The last part of the battle is fought with assault rifles, LSWs and grenades; in the case of the Gurkhas the famous kukri chopping knife may be used in close-quarter combat. The platoon structure is now broken up and the three sections of each platoon act independently, each of them fielding two half-sections of four soldiers, who form two fire teams. If needed, the reserve can be used to support elements of the attacking force, to respond to enemy counter-attacks or engage unexpected enemy positions.

Another possible type of mission is to drop troops directly into battle by helicopter to support engaged troops. For transport in helicopters the soldiers are divided into "chalks" each of a certain number of "pax" (passenger and equipment); e.g., planning figures for a distance of 120km are 24 pax for a Chinook, 12 for a Puma and six for a Lynx. Normally the equipment a single soldier carries on operations allows him to fight without resupply for 48 hours. The British Army uses the "mission command principle", whereby individual soldiers and junior leaders, who have a high level of basic skills and are well trained in teamwork, are given a task to fulfill and will then make their own plans, making use of the available resources to achieve the best possible result. This approach is the basis for success in the airmobile role, where troops operating far from their Forward Line of Own Troops and enjoying limited support have to react quickly to changing situations.

(Above) While the chalk commander raises the orange card to show the pilot where to land, the six infantrymen await the order to board the Lynx Mk.9. Boarding procedure is for the first men to reach the aircraft to open the doors – on one side this is usually the chalk commander. Then the rest get aboard, the last to enter being the chalk commander, who hands his orange card to the crew and closes the door.

(Left) Once they are operational in the field, airmobile soldiers mostly have to carry all their equipment on their backs and march to their objective the hard way. Here a Gurkha leaves the HLS with 30lbs of Milan ATGW firing post on top of his bergen. The bergen usually accomodates the sleeping bag, washing and eating kit, spare clothing and boots, waterproofs and NBC kit, ammunition, rations, plus any small personal belongings.

(Opposite) A half-section of four soldiers take cover in a ditch while they await the order to advance. They are equipped with L85A1, LSW and LAW 80. In the foreground Corporal Yog, a section commander in B Coy 1 RS, is wearing a so-called "SAS type" hooded smock. Note the rank patch on his helmet cover and the signal whistle on his PLCE yoke. The L85A1 assault rifle, also known as SA80, is a gas operated 5.56mm calibre weapon weighing 5.08kg (11lbs) complete with 30 round magazine and SUSAT sights. It can be fired single shot, or fully automatic at a rate of fire between 610 and 770rpm, to an effective range of 500m.

(Opposite inset) A happy warrior of B Coy, 1 RS wearing a cap comforter; note that he wears body armour. Most infantrymen are trained in a second skill, e.g. driver, assault pioneer, radio operator, mortarman, etc.

3 & 4 Regiments, Army Air Corps

The brigade's aviation asset is formed by 3 and 4 Regiments, Army Air Corps. These units are equally structured, and are currently based at Wattisham airfield in Suffolk. Each regiment fields two anti-tank squadrons (3rd Regt, 662 and 663 Sqns; 4th Regt, 654 and 669 Sqns) and one LBH, light battlefield helicopter squadron (3rd Regt, 653 Sqn; 4th Regt, 659 Squadron), as well as an HQ and support squadron and a REME workshop.

Each of the anti-tank squadrons fields six Lynx Mk.7 helicopters, as well as six Gazelles which can be used as FAC (Forward Air Control) helicopters for "fast air" (i.e. jet ground attack), or as AOPs (Airborne Observation Posts) for artillery and mortars. For these tasks the Gazelles are equipped with laser target markers.

The Lynx antitank helicopters provide the combat power of the AAC regiments. In the anti-armour battle they normally operate in pairs, guided by a Gazelle working as a spotter. The TOW anti-tank missile system has an effective range from 50m to 3750m. Two Gazelles and one Lynx Mk.7 can form an Aviation Recce Patrol (ARP), which covers between 5km and 7km of the brigade's front. In battle each squadron can provide two AOPs or one ARP for 24 hours a day, subject to maintenance periods and available crews. During daylight deployment of brigade combat elements into enemy territory by helicopters of the SHF, the anti-tank helicopters often form a protective screen against enemy forces.

The LBH squadrons (nicknamed "Night Hawks", 659 Sqn, and "Pink Panthers", 653 Sqn) are each equipped with 11 x Lynx Mk.9. These are used to move small groups of soldiers around the battlefield. The Lynx Mk.9 has a maximum load of 5125kg (11,275lbs) in contrast to the Mk.7's payload of 4875kg (10,725lbs). This means that the Mk.7 can usually transport two to three soldiers with full equipment in addition to the fuel, while the Mk.9 can carry up to six. Fuel capacity gives two hours of flying, which means up to 450km (280 miles) in range.

Using image-intensified night vision systems most LBH missions are carried out at night, e.g. to insert infantry under the cover of darkness to establish a recce screen around a planned fire base, HLS or FARP. Once this is secure the main body will fly in with the SHF. The crews specialise in night flying and normally operate at ground level in close formation with a distance of 25m to 50m between the helicopters. During this mission the night vision equipment is used in co-ordination with station keeping lights (SKL) which can only be seen with the night vision equipment and are invisible to the naked eye.

The sky over a battlefield is an extremely hazardous place, where the electronic eyes of "friendly" and enemy air defences constantly rove in search of prey. For this reason the complete airspace is ruled by the Airspace Control Order (ACO) which is renewed every eight hours. Mainly it consists of Air Control Points (ACP), fixed locations on the map which link up to form the Aviation Flight Routes from the operational base (also known as Sky Blue One) to the commital area. Along the Aviation Flight Routes the air defence assets of the brigade protect the helicopters against enemy air strikes. In addition the ACO co-ordinates flying levels for rotary aircraft and fast jets, and contains frequencies and tactical information.

Leaving Sky Blue One, the helicopters fly from ACP to ACP up to the "in gate", the entrance to the commital area. From

(Opposite) A Lynx Mk.7 fitted wih TOW anti-tank guided weapons hovers over a potential new FOB while the aviation battle group commander coordinates the ground units' defences.

(Above) The co-pilot, who normally assists the pilot with navigation and communications.

Here he is looking through the roof-mounted, stabilized M65 sight. All he needs to do after a TOW missile is fired is to keep the aiming mark on the target by using the joystick, and the SACLOS guidance system will transmit the flight path corrections to the missile over two guidance wires.

here they choose their way freely, considering the tactical situation and the needs of their particular task. Once this task is achieved they leave the commital area through the "out gate", and again follow the line of ACPs back to Sky Blue One. If required, the Tactical Supply Wing (TSW) can establish a Main Refueling Area along the route or a FARP (Forward Arming & Refueling Point) directly in the commital area.

During an air transport mission the drop-off point in the commital area is usually called Sky Blue Two. It can easily be converted into another Forward Operation Base; if this is done it is renamed Sky Blue One and the former Sky Blue One forms the new staging area. To establish and secure a new FOB usually requires 18 Puma and Chinook loads to carry the ground elements of the aviation battle group, including the aviation company of one of the brigade's infantry battalions, an artillery battery with six light guns, the TAC group, battery command post and three FOO parties, engineer and air defence elements as well as the forward repair team, airportable fuel containers, part

of the Tactical Supply Wing, and the battle group's "fly forward" command post. The deployment will take four hours; another four are needed to dig the unit in to stage one. All resources for 48 hours' unsupported operations are carried by the aviation battle group.

In addition to their helicopters, each flying squadron includes a signal section with three Land Rover FFRs; an MT section with two motorbikes, two GS Land Rovers, one petrol, oil and lubrication truck, one truck vehicle mechanic REME, one fire truck, and ten tactical air-refuelers (TAR), as well as an admin section with a 1-ton truck and a Land Rover.

The regimental HQ Squadron comprises all administrative and logistic elements: a quartermaster (admin) section, a quartermaster (technical) section, the command troop, an MT troop, a regimental aid post, catering section, FAACO and pay section. The regiment also has a REME Workshop for first-line helicopter maintenance, which is divided into two anti-tank squadron maintenance sections and an LBH maintenance section. Including all these elements, each regiment numbers 34 officers and 338 other ranks.

(Opposite, top) A Lynx Mk.7 of 654 Sqn, 4 Regt AAC has just fired one of its eight TOW 2B (Tubelaunched, Opticallytracked, Wireguided) missiles. The TOW 2B shaped charge high explosive armour piercing warhead weighs 3.9kg (8.58lbs); it can penetrate armour up to 800mm (31ins) at a maximum range of 3750m. The British Army's TOW are being up-graded under the Further Improved TOW Programme which will increase penetration and range. (Photo courtesy GKN Westland Helicopters)

(Opposite) During an exercise Army Air Corps Lynx Mk.7s are refueled and rearmed with TOW missiles at a FARP; in battle this is carried out with running engines to save time. If the FARP is no further than 10km (6.25 miles) from the action, then it does not normally take longer than 15 minutes to reach the FARP, load eight new TOWs, refuel and fly back into battle.

(Above) A member of the REME Workshop of one of the AAC regiments carries out routine checks on a Lynx Mk.9 LBH after a certain number of flying hours. Random checks provide security, preventing function failures and accidents resulting from technical failures.

(Above right) A Lynx Mk.9 LBH is refueled at a FARP before leaving for another mission.

(Right) The two-man crew of a Lynx Mk.9 LBH carry out pre-flight checks before taking off to lift soldiers of the aviation infantry company back to the FOB. Note the green and red slide on the shoulder straps, the 24 Airmobile Brigade patch worn on both shoulders, and helmet details. The slide was introduced by LtCol Volkers, CO of 4 Regt AAC, to distinguish his personnel from those of 9 Regt when the two were based together at Detmold.

(Above & left) Lynx Mk.7s photographed during operations as part of SFOR in Bosnia in April 1997. The GPMG mounted in the side sliding door is manned by an additional crew member wearing a flight crew helmet connected to the helicopter''s intercom system. Note that the TOW missile launchers have been dismounted. In Bosnia this configuration of the Lynx is used as a VIP transport and liaison helicopter between the large number of British SFOR bases. The Lynx Mk.7 is powered by two Rolls Royce GEM 411 engines developing 1120hp each. Maximum speed is 259km/h (120mph) and maximum range 634km (394 miles) with a fuel load of 973 litres. Maximum take-off weight is 4763kg (10,478lbs).

(Opposite, top) This Gazelle AH1 belongs to 654 Sqn of 4 Regt AAC. Used as a platform for Forward Air Controllers or as an Airborne Observation Post, the Gazelle has a maximum speed of 265km/h (124mph) and is powered by a Turbomeca/ RollsRoyce Astazou 111N engine. Maximum take-off weight is 1.8 tons; a fuel capacity of 445 litres gives a range of 670km (416 miles). In the anti-armour battle two Lynx Mk.7 TOW operate together with a Gazelle acting as recce and control platform, from which a section commander directs the anti-tank helicopters to their targets without the enemy being aware of them until the last moment. When the Lynxes have to break off for the FARP the Gazelle keeps contact, ready to give new targets as soon as the rearmed Lynxes return.

(Right) Four of the 11 Lynx Mk.9s of 653 Sqn, 3 Regt AAC. The Lynx Mk.9 Light Battlefield Helicopter is an upgraded version of the Mk.7 with a 250kg (550lb) greater payload. It also has improved avionics, an upgraded RollsRoyce GEM 42 powerpack and new rotor blades, allowing the Mk.9 to fly at night at very low level in close formation. The most visible external difference, however, is simply the use of wheeled landing gear instead of the skids of the Mk.7.

19 Regiment, Royal Artillery

The Highland gunners of 19 Regiment Royal Artillery are among the brigade's most experienced units in airmobile operations. During the time it was based at Dortmund in Germany it formed part of 6 Airmobile Brigade; after it returned to the UK the regiment came under 24 Airmobile Brigade command at the time when the brigade was based at Catterick. Today the regiment consists of three regular gun batteries – 25/170 (Imjin), 28/143 (Tombs' Troop), and 2/51 (Kabul); one TA battery – 269 (West Riding Volunteers); and 13 (Martinique 1809) Headquarters Battery. Each of the four gun batteries can field six Royal Ordnance 105mm Light Guns, towed by Steyr "Pinzgauer" 718M trucks which also carry the six-man crews, ammunition and all necessary equipment.

The batteries and the command and control elements, which use FACE (Field Artillery Computer Equipment) to process target information from the Forward Observation Officer (FOO) teams to issue fire orders, are collectively called the Gun Group. The second element is the TAC Group, consisting of three FOO teams and the Fire Planning Cell. The FPC is the battery commander's party, which is usually attached to the battle group HQ to assist the battle group commander and co-ordinate fire support.

Each of the four-man FOO teams is attached to a company or squadron of the battle group, calling in artillery support as needed. The artillery fire is then directed by the FOO team; for this task they can employ OTIS (Observation Thermal Imaging System), LRF (Laser Range Finder), and MSTAR (Manportable Surveillance Target Acquisition Radar).

13 HQ Battery is responsible for the logistic support of the gun batteries and also delivers overall command and support. Headed by 19 Regiment's commanding officer, the regimental HQ runs the Fire Support Co-ordination Cell inside the brigade HQ, which co-ordinates all the brigade's indirect fire as well as all brigade reconnaissance and targeting assets. The regiment's Light Aid Detachment REME is also part of the HQ battery, as well as the support element responsible for all adminstrative work and supplies of ammunition, food, fuel, etc. Altogether the regiment fields 34 officers and 350 other ranks and a total of 147 wheeled vehicles and 84 trailers.

During airmobile operations, e.g. a raid on an enemy stronghold, the battle group's artillery asset is usually deployed by helicopter to establish a fire base (FB) and support the attack of the infantry and anti-tank helicopters with indirect fire. "Indirect" fire is fired from one point but controlled or directed by an observer from another position – the firing artillerymen cannot see the target. First the gun position officer (GPO) and his team will be flown in by Puma or Lynx to survey the position and mark the location for each gun. This is necessary to ensure the highest accuracy of fire – a calculation which also factors in such variables as wind direction and speed, ambient and charge temperatures, etc.

Shortly after the GPO the battery's control and command element arrive. They will process the target information together with the "own grid" and other necessary data for a fire command, including type of round, type of charge, number of rounds, bearing and elevation. To speed up the process

"Gunzon", a slightly smaller version of the vehicle-mounted FACE, is used if vehicles cannot be taken to the gun position.

Next to be flown in are the gun detachments, each gun with its crew and the equipment necessary to establish and camouflage a gun position. The gun can be carried by either a Puma or a Chinook as an underslung load, or by a Chinook as an internal load, the choice depending on the tactical situation. For an operation deep in enemy territory the guns are usually flown as internal loads, since this enables the Chinook pilots to fly faster and at very low altitude, presenting a more difficult target for enemy anti-aircraft defences. On the other hand, landing to unload a gun takes several minutes, while just unhooking an underslung load takes only seconds, and thus allows a faster rotation of the aircraft to pick up another load.

At the fire base the incoming helicopter will be directed to the marked position for that gun and drop or unload it as close as possible – without a towing vehicle the gun crew can only manhandle the gun for short distances, depending on the ground. Once the weapon is in place the crews immediately make their guns ready to fire, preparing the ammunition and camouflaging the position. When the fire missions are completed the battery will redepoy as soon as possible to avoid enemy counter-battery. In this case guns are normally lifted as underslung loads to speed up the process. Directly the last round is on its way the guns are rigged up for slinging, and the fire position is transformed into a helicopter pick-up point.

If necessary the complete gun batteries and their equipment as well as all essential elements of the HQ battery can be transported forward by helicopter to support the brigade's operation. The heavier vehicles of the regiment, including a Foden recovery vehicle and several 4-ton trucks and ammunition transporters, will follow later by road.

(**Opposite**) The Gun Position Officer is flown in by Lynx, and he and his team measure the position and mark the points where the helicopters are to drop the guns. Here a GPO uses the L1A1 Director Artillery; the location is pinpointed by measuring angles to landscape features, by reference to the magnetic meridian or by astronomical observations. The exact location of the director can then be used by the individual guns as a datum point to offset their bearings when engaging a target.

(**Left**) Deploying to a fire base deep in enemy territory, a 105mm Light Gun is unloaded from an RAF Chinook. The crew left the aircraft first, loaded down with ammunition, camouflage equipment, gun sights and other necessary equipment. Depending on the ground and weather, moving a gun around can be hard work; the helicopters are guided as close as possible to the final gun position.

(**Below**) Gunners hastily prepare for a fire mission.While No.3 is laying the gun, Nos.5, 6, 4 and 2 prepare shells and charges and No.1 co-ordinates their efforts. Note the wheel attachment in the foreground; if the gun is carried as an internal load this is fixed to the trail end spade to make it easier to roll it down the helicopter's rear ramp.

KABUL 1842

(Below) The guns of 19 Regt's three Regular batteries bear on the left side battery badges tracing their historical lineage to RA units which have distinguished themselves in battle over three centuries. That of 2/51 (Kabul) Bty recalls the heroism of British gunners during the disastrous First Afghan War.

(Above left) The battery's command element use "Gunzon", a handheld fire data computer, to speed up the process of developing fire orders. Gunzon is fed with all necessary data about the target, own position, weather and temperatures,from which the bearing, elevation and charge are calculated. Once the fire mission is given the battery will fire one or two test rounds. The FOO will observe the fall of shot; if necessary a correction is given, and the battery opens "fire for effect". The target and location data can either be taken from a map or by GPS and laser rangefinders. Note the first lieutenant's helmet ranking.

(Above right) Minutes after the gun has been unloaded from the helicopter the crew No.3 checks measurements to the director's location using the gun laying system. The speed with which guns can be brought into action is a key factor in the airmobile role. Note the badge of 28/143 Bty (Tombs' Troop), its sphinx and tiger recalling service in Egypt during the Napoleonic Wars and later in India.

(Opposite) "Fire mission, bearing 1824 mils, elevation 442 mils, two rounds, fire for effect!" When the order reaches the gun crew, No.3 lays the gun on the correct elevation and bearing; No.4 loads the shell, which is rammed by No.2 before No.4 loads the case and closes the breech block. No.1, the gun commander, signals "Ready" to the battery CP, and awaits the order "Fire!". The 105mm Light Gun can engage targets out to 17.2km (10.68 miles). Ammunition consists of a shell (smoke, illumination, HE, HESH or smoke marker) and a separate cased charge. The charges comes in different strengths for different ranges, colour coded for easy recognition:

Charge 1 (red): 2.5 5.7km
Charge 2 (white): 2.7 7.2km
Charge 3 (blue): 5.9 9.5km
Charge 4 (orange): 7.9 12.2km
Charge 4 (red, white, orange
    & green): 8.7 to 13.6km
Charge 5 (green maximum, all
    together): 15.3km

The smaller charges are combined for the required range; there is also a single Charge 6, in a different case, which can reach up to 17.2km.

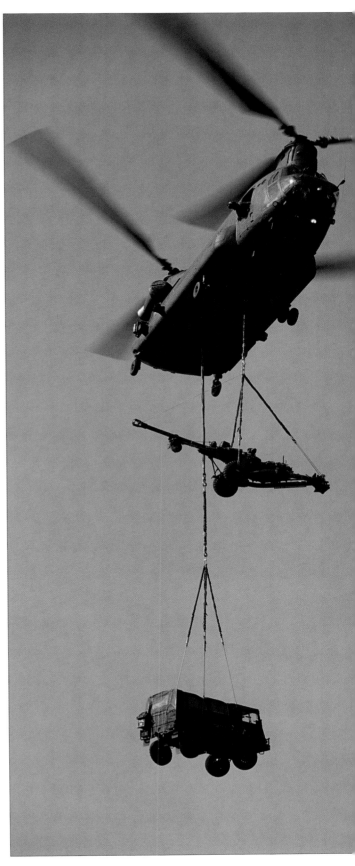

(Opposite, top) A gunner of 25/170 (Imjin) Bty lays his L118A1 105mm Light Gun during deployment with UN "Task Force Alpha" on Mt Igman, Bosnia, from 23 July 1995; note the blue helmet cover and white painted gun. The tiger battery badge and scroll recall the part played by Royal Artillery gunners in the desperate defence of the Imjin River line in Korea during the Chinese Communist offensive of April 1951. (Photo courtesy Yves Debay)

(Left) The guns are towed by the Steyr 716M Pinzgauer, known in the British Army as Truck or Utility Medium (Heavy Duty) TUM(HD). This 4x4 vehicle has a combat load of 3.85 tons; it can carry up to 1400kg (3,080lbs) and tow loads of up to 1900kg (4,180lbs). The 2.4 litre 6-cylinder engine gives a top road speed of 122km/h (75mph). Its off-road capabilities include a safe fording depth of 70cm (27.5ins), ground clearance of 34cm (13.4ins) and an approach angle of 40 degrees. The

Pinzgauer is used both as a gun/crew and battery command post vehicle, and in the FFR role.

(Above) After a fire mission gunners of 28/143 (Tombs' Troop) Bty prepare their guns to be picked up by helicopter. Note the red velcro ties around the harness to prevent it from twisting; as the gun is lifted these pull open in sequence. The rigging of guns has to be completed at great speed, but requires special care because the harness can easily get snagged or twisted, with dangerous consequences.

(Right) With its huge load capacity of 8164kg (17,960lbs) the RAF"s Chinook HC2 can transport a 3850kg TUM(HD) with a 1858kg 105mm gun (8,470lbs plus 4,087lbs) as underslung loads, together with the six-man crew and their equipment as internal load. To move a complete battery with all necessary equipment and ammunition to fulfill a fire mission takes ten Chinook loads.

Brigade Headquarters & 210 Signal Squadron

From Brigade HQ the brigade commander directs the units of 24 Airmobile in battle, supported by the brigade staff and the 130 all ranks of 210 Signal Squadron. "Brigade Main", as the HQ is called when deployed in battle, is usually sited in a farm, abandoned factory or similar buildings which offer the vehicles some measure of protection from enemy reconnaissance and the weather. All necessary equipment to establish the headquarters, including tents, radio equipment, computers and power generators, can be stowed in four Land Rovers FFR with trailers; and a team of eight soldiers can set it up and camouflage it in approximately one hour. 24 Airmobile Brigade HQ and Signal Squadron is divided into A, B, and Support Troops. A Troop comprises a brigade HQ section, the TAC HQ with two Land Rover FFR, four radio re-broadcast stations for secure HF communication, two multinational link detachments and two ZIPOs (Zone Indicating Point Officers) of the RAF. ZIPOs give flag signals to aircraft during radio silence, and are usually placed at the FOB (ZIPO Forward) and staging area (ZIPO Rear). B Troop consists of a second brigade HQ section, three liaison officer teams with Land Rovers FFR, and the Brigade Support Group (Rear) section with trunk and line communication systems. The Support Troop consists of the quartermaster section with the echelon, usually placed at BSG(R); a light aid detachment REME; and the Regimental Sergeant Major section. Altogether 210 Signal Squadron's vehicle park consists of five motorcycles, 20 Land Rovers 90 and 110 FFR, eight Land Rovers GS and eight Bedford 4-ton trucks.

The Brigade Main HQ itself is usually situated in a large tent or other shelter with two "Bird tables" in the middle for current operations and future plans. All important information relevant to the brigade's battle is noted on maps or tables. Around these tables so-called "cells" of all the brigade's elements are placed with all necessary communications and computer equipment, so that they can advise the brigade commander and his chief of staff on possibilities and situations. All new information on the current battle arrives in the HQ through the Brigade Operations Desk via loudspeaker; Ops Desk watchkeepers transfer it to the Bird table.

The cells in Brigade Main are as follows:

Artillery Operations

G3 (also called Main or Ops Desk)

Coms Ops (signals)

RMP Desk

G4 (Equipment Support & Supply and Medical Support)

G2 (Intelligence)

Engineer Operations

NBC & Air Defence

Air Operations (run by RAF personnel, including BASO, BALO/SH and BALO/OS; co-ordinates Joint Air Ground (JAG) Operations with the Army Air Corps)

G1 (Personnel and Casualty Reporting)

(Above) The busy "watchkeepers" at the Ops Desk, where the decisions of the Operations Officer are transformed into orders and passed down to the brigade's combat units; and reports received from the battlefield are transferred to the "Bird tables". In the modern HQ computers are used in a variety of roles to minimize time schedules.

(Opposite, top) All the radio equipment of Brigade HQ and 210 Signal Sqn is installed inside Land Rovers to allow easy transport by helicopter. The signaler in the back of this Land Rover 110 FFR is operating the VRC 353, which is used on the brigade command net on a frequency range from 30 to 75.975 MHz for voice and telegraph communication in VHF/FM. Note the blue and white diamond-shaped flash of 210 Squadron.

(Right) All information which needs to be factored into future operations planning is noted on the Bird table. Here HQ personnel mark enemy positions while staff officers discuss procedures for the next task. In the background a scarlet beret identifies the Royal Military Police Desk. Here all orders for convoys throughout the brigade's area of responsibility are developed in concert with the G1 and G4 cells, and information on the condition and status of all roads is collated. Note the rifle within reach of the female RMP soldier – even in the HQ complex everybody keeps personal weapons to hand.

A camouflaged Land Rover 110 FFR of the Step-Up HQ prepared for movement as internal load in a Chinook, and a despatch rider on his Harley Davidson, awaiting the arrival of the helicopter.

When the Ops Officer has discussed the latest situation with the responsible cells (e.g. artillery, air cell and engineers, for the preparation of a defensive battle) the watchkeepers transform his decisions into orders for the units involved. Here the communications cell comes into play, ensuring that every element of the brigade HQ gets the necessary communication lines to work successfully. For this purpose 210 Signal Squadron establish and maintain the following communication systems:

Brigade Command Net – secure VHF, between the staging area and the battle groups, engineers, etc., using Clansman radios PRC 320, VRC 321, VRC 322 and VRC 353.

Brigade Logistic Net – insecure HF, between all logistic elements including BSG (Rear) and BSG (Forward). On this net Kipling is used, a new logistic data computer system.

Command Net – insecure HF, similar to the Brigade Command Net.

Line System – inside the staging area for telephone and fax communication. This is drawn by the signal detachments of the battle groups and maintained by 210 Signal Squadron. The system is also connected to the civilian telecommunication lines of the host nation.

To link up 24 Airmobile Brigade with higher command structures, e.g. a British Division HQ, HQ MND(C) or HQ ARRC, coms are normally supplied from top to bottom: i.e., in the case of MND(C), 11 Dutch Signal Bn will establish a Zodiac net; or, in case of national deployment, a British signal regiment will connect the brigade via Ptarmigan. Ptarmigan provides data, telegraph, voice and fax communications, and consists of a network of electronic exchanges or trunk switches to connect multichannel radio and satellite relays. With Ptarmigan it is possible to give an isolated or mobile user an entry point into the entire system by using the "single channel radio access". Ptarmigan on brigade and battle group level can be linked up via SATCOM with another Ptarmigan area, e.g. staging area or Forward Operation Base. When operating with other European nations Euromax can be used, a system similar to Ptarmigan.

From 30 Signal Regiment at Bramcote detachments are attached under 210 Signal Squadron command which support the brigade with TAC SAT when operating with UK national assets, and with SATCOM which can link up with Ptarmigan and Euromax on multinational operations. For this purpose the Skynet 4B system is used to link headquarters with the UK. For communication with the RAF, 21 Signal Regiment attaches one platoon (normally 1st Pltn, 135 Coy) under 24 Airmobile Brigade command.

Inside the HQ, A TAC CS (Army Tactical Computer System) is used; this runs on MicroSoft Office and links up all cells for quicker information exchange. In 1998 it is planned to introduce a Local Area Network which can connect to Ptarmigan, giving the opportunity to E-mail information to other locations. The new software will include specially designed programmes for G2/G3 battle planning operations (GP3) and G1/G4 stores and logistic applications (QP24).

During changes of position the HQ staff are transferred to an established "Alternative HQ", which then becomes Brigade Main. If the fast-moving battle requires it, a TAC HQ can be deployed forward on to the battlefield. It is possible to remove TAC immediately after the situation is cleared, or to change TAC into Main after TAC is fully established. If the latter option is chosen the current Main will be closed down and flown forward to meet up with TAC. To insert TAC, which is also known as "Step-Up", three Chinooks are needed. After Ptarmigan access is established, artillery coms and brigade command net can be used; key staff are flown in, including the brigade commander, OC artillery, OC engineers and SO3 G3.

Support Helicopter Force

The main function of the Support Helicopter Force HQ at RAF Benson is to co-ordinate RAF support to the Army by providing tactical airmobility and logistic lift. During times of crisis 5 Airborne and 24 Airmobile Brigades have priority for calls upon the Support Helicopter Force squadrons.

Today the SHF consists of three Chinook squadrons (Nos.7, 18 and 27, each equipped with 12 new Chinook HC2 purchased from the USA and all based at RAF Odiham); and two squadrons (No.33 based at RAF Benson and No.230 at RAF Aldergrove), each with 12 Puma HC1. There is an additional squadron with 15 Wessex HC2 aircraft (No.72, from RAF Aldergrove). All squadrons are equally structured and consist of two flights with six helicopters each, a command and support element and a workshop. In the future No.28 Sqn from RAF Benson, also part of the SHF and up to now equipped with the elderly Wessex, will be the first squadron to receive the new British transport helicopter EH 101 Merlin; it is planned that the unit will be operational in around the year 2000.

During times of crisis HQ SHF acts as an independent element of the Royal Air Force, which on request can be colocated for a certain time with 24 Airmobile Brigade HQ when helicopter support is needed to fulfill the brigade's task. Commanded by the Brigade Air Staff Officer – a squadron leader who also advises the brigade commander on questions concerning the RAF – the Brigade Air Cell consists of the Brigade Air Liaison Officer/Operational Support (BALO/OS) and the Brigade Air Liaison Officer/Support Helicopter (BALO/SH).

The latter links up with HQ SHF to place the request for the needed helicopter capacity. This figure is calculated from the brigade battle group's air movement plans once the ground units are given their objectives. It is submitted to the Brigade Air Cell which co-ordinates support helicopters, AAC aviation and fast jet operations. Depending on the scale of the needed SH capacity, helicopters are either attached for a short period, or a small HQ and helicopter units can be colocated with Brigade HQ (and come partly under its command) for the duration of the operation. For this reason, during operations the RAF SHF HQ is on six hours' notice to move if a new brigade task is given – the same period of notice as Brigade HQ. Once the task is fulfilled the RAF element can be redeployed, e.g. attached to 5 Airborne Bde or other Army or Commando units to support their missions. For large scale operations it is estimated that at least 18 Chinooks and Pumas of the various squadrons will be used to support the brigade.

Together with the squadrons, logistical and administrative units will also be attached. Among these are the Tactical Supply Wing from RAF Stafford with their fuel tankers, dealing with all fuel aspects including the establishment of FARPs for the SHF. The unit's equipment includes air refueling tanks and pumps which can be flown forward inside Chinooks. Other units are MAOTs (Mobile Air Operation Teams) which work as a link between Army ground forces and the support helicopters. For

(Above) An RAF sergeant loadmaster of a Chinook crew gives a good view of aircrew equipment. The flight crew helmet has an integrated communication system; it is necessary to protect his ears from the hellish noise, and his eyes with a fibreglass visor. Over his flying suit he wears a survival vest.

(Left) The right sleeve patch of the JHSU, which provides riggers for transport helicopters.

transporting both underslung and internal loads special rigging equipment is stored, maintained and provided by the Joint Helicopter Support Unit; the JHSU also prepares loads, vehicles and personnel for air movement. For larger scale CASEVAC operations the specially trained personnel of the Tactical Medical Wing are available. As weather can be a major factor in the airmobile scenario there also is a mobile meteorological unit

under SHF HQ. To link up all the RAF elements, 21 Signal Regiment provides communication lines between ground and air units, refueling points, MAOTs, locations, etc. Last but not least, the RAF also provide their own mobile catering unit.

During an operation a HelQuest from a battle group or other unit is given to the Brigade Air Cell. Here it is checked with HQ SHF to find out whether capacity is available, either from AAC or RAF helicopters or a combination of both. Then a HelTask is given by HQ SHF to the support helicopter crews, including information on frequencies, pick-up and drop points, tactical scenario, loads, and the AOP.

Once the helicopters are at the given pick-up point they are guided to their loads by the main marshaller in the LZ, sometimes nicknamed "the beachmaster". They are awaited at the load itself by a sub-marshaller. First the helicopters touch down to pick up "chalks" of troops. Once the chalk is on board the pilot takes off and picks up an underslung load. Following the details given by the chalk commander's orange card (see page 11) and the brigade's AOP, the pilots fly the troops and their equipment to the planned HLS, and after the load is dropped they proceed to fulfill their next task.

From May 1960 the SHF HQ was based at RAF Odiham; in that month No.225 Sqn arrived with Sycamores and Whirlwinds. Since then Odiham has seen the Wessex, Belvedere, Puma and Chinook enter service; and has been the departure point for helicopter deployments to operational theatres such as Malaysia,

Borneo, Cyprus, the Lebanon, Northern Ireland, Zimbabwe, Belize, the Falklands, the Gulf and Northern Iraq. The current peacetime commitments of the SHF are extensive. The Wessex, which first entered service in 1964, continues to give valuable support in Northern Ireland and Cyprus, and Chinooks remain stationed in the Falklands and Northern Ireland. Elements of the SHF are also on rotation to support the Multinational Division (South-West) of SFOR (previously IFOR) in Bosnia.

* * *

In addition to transport capacity, the Royal Air Force is ready to provide offensive and defensive support to 24 Airmobile Brigade, employing the available range of fighter/ ground attack jets in a variety of roles including reconnaissance, attack on ground targets and protection against enemy aircraft.

When RAF fighter aircraft provide close support to the brigade's combat elements they are guided by Tactical Air Control Parties from the Army. There are two under brigade command, 615 and 616 TACP. Each of these breaks down into two Forward Air Contoller teams of two soldiers. The FACs are equipped with laser target markers and all necessary surveillance and communication equipment to guide pilots to their targets. In many cases the target is marked with a laser or infrared aiming device (IRAD-8000), the signals from which are picked up by the electronics of the aircraft, arm the bombs, and guide them into their targets. With IRAD-8000 the FAC team can mark targets between 800m and 1200m away from its own position.

(Opposite, top) Puma HC1 of No.33 Sqn from RAF Odiham. With a crew of three (pilot, co-pilot and loadmaster) this workhorse of the SHF can carry 12 to 16 fully equipped troops, or six stretchers and six sitting casualties. Two Turbomeca 111C4 turbines give a cruising speed of about 258km/h (160mph). With a maximum take-off load of 7400kg (16,280lbs) including 3200kg underslung (7,040lbs), the operational range – i.e. to reach an HLS, drop off a load and return safely to a FARP – is around 120km (75 miles). This range was used as the planning base for the British airmobile concept.

(Above) At the time of writing it is planned to deliver the first of 22 Merlin HC Mk3 utility helicopters to the SHF in late 1999, delivery to be completed in late 2001. Three RTM 32202/8 engines with integral inlet particle separators and anti-icing provide improved safety and survivability. The Lightweight Common Control Unit (LWCCU) by Racal gives increased reliability and maintainability for the crew interface with the aircraft's mission, tactical, navigation and communication systems. Merlin can carry 30 equipped troops, 16 stretchers, or bulky freight like an LSV. Maximum take-off weight is 14600kg (32,120lbs), giving underslung loads up to 5443kg (11,975lbs). A machine gun position can be mounted in the large sliding side door. Production is by Augusta and GKN Westland Helicopters. (Photo courtesy GKN Westland Helicopters Ltd.)

(Right) A Forward Air Control team from 615 TACP observe the attack of two RAF Tornadoes on an "enemy" position. Note the IRAD-8000 mounted on the second man's rifle. The team member in the foreground holds radio contact with the aircraft while his collegue observes the impact.

(**Left**) A Land Rover FFR is guided into the tail of a Chinook by the RAF loadmaster. The rear ramp is 1.98m high by 2.31m wide (6ft 6ins x7ft 6ins), which allows the loading of light vehicles and bulky stores. The tandem rotors of the Chinook HC2 are powered by two AVCO Lycoming T55 L11E engines which give a cruising speed of 270km/h (167mph).

(**Above**) Chinooks of the SHF pick up Land Rover 110 Defenders as underslung loads during an airmobile infantry move forward to a new FOB. The vehicles are lined up in rows; the helicopter touches down in front of the row, picks up internal loads (e.g. a second Land Rover or a chalk of troops); then passes along the prepared loads and picks up the last in the line. Not visible in this photograph is the main marshaller who guides the helicopters to their loads. In the rear row a sub-marshaller can be spotted among a hooking party by his high visibility armbands.

(**Above**) Chinook HC2 about to lift an underslung Land Rover and trailer, under the guidance of a sub-marshaller with luminous red armbands. With a crew of four (pilot, co-pilot, navigator and loadmaster) the Chinook can transport 36 fully equipped troops or 24 stretcher casualties. This capacity can be extended on operations, when peacetime safety limits do not apply; then the load can be up to 10 tons or 50 passengers (and there is a hair raising legend from the Falklands War which makes even that look tame...). With a full load of fuel and maximum payload the range is greatly reduced.

(**Right**) Underslung loads can be lifted on three cargo hooks; here pallets of ammunition are flown in to the CSS Bn distribution point. The brigade's main front line vehicles – Land Rovers, ATMPs and GMWPs – can all be carried as internal loads. After the upgrade to HC2 (US CH47D) standard, improvements including infrared jammers, missile approach warning indicators, chaff and flare dispensers, a long range fuel system and machine gun mounts give the helicopter greater survivability.

41

51 Field Squadron, Royal Engineers

(Left) Abseiling from helicopters enables the sappers to get into difficult areas where landing is impractical. The typical mission would be to abseil in with mines or explosives to prepare obstacles in the path of an advancing enemy force, or to slow down a counter-attack while the brigade prepared its main defensive plan.

(Right) A sapper team member uses detonation cord to link up a number of charges No.1 6in Mk.6 to blow up a bridge – just one of a variety of types of charge which enable 51 Sqn to deal efficiently with any target.

This unit has a peacetime strength of 210 all ranks, increased to 275 personnel under war conditions. The squadron is based in Ripon, North Yorkshire, near the former 24 Airmobile Brigade base at Catterick. The unit is structured in four Field Troops each 32 men strong, equipped with three Land Rovers and a 4-ton DAF truck; HQ Troop, Plant Troop, Resources Troop, Motor Transport & Echelon Troop, and a Forward Repair Team REME. Altogether the unit fields 120 vehicles, from Land Rovers up to Combat Engineer Tractors (CET), of which four can be found in the vehicle park. The total also includes four ATMPs, five GCBs, two Medium Wheeled Tractors and two Ultralight Wheeled Tractors. Mineclearing equipment, mobile power tools such as chain saws, breakers and metalcutters, pumps and lighting sets are among the unit's large and varied equipment stores, allowing it to fulfill the complete range of military engineering support tasks. This includes close engineering support to the fighting echelon as well as general engineering support for the brigade's daily life in war and peace.

Close engineer support consists mainly of three tasks: support for mobility, counter-mobility operations, and survival support. Support for mobility is provided by building bridges and roads, establishing minefield breaches, minefield clearance and EOD (Explosive Ordnance Disposal). Conversely, counter-mobility tasks include mine laying, route cratering, obstacle construction (e.g. anti-tank ditches) and demolition. The mines laid are now limited to anti-tank mines; Great Britain no longer uses anti-personnel mines – but as the enemy probably will, the engineers are of course still highly trained to meet this threat. For certain missions specialists of the unit can also be drawn together to form diving teams or EOD teams. Survival support covers, e.g., digging gun pits for the artillery and trenches for the infantry, building field fortifications, and armed plant support with the squadron's CETs. The list of general support missions for 24 Airmobile Brigade features water supply, infrastructure engineering, plant, electrical engineering, camp set-up (as in the tent city of a staging area), building and maintaining roads, constructing the BFI, and general artisan support down to painting and decorating.

Depending on the specific task given to the brigade and on the results of an advance recce by engineer or other officers of the brigade's advance party, 51 Fd Sqn RE can order at need various heavy equipment that is not found in their own stores from RE equipment pools or depots. This might include e.g. boats, cranes such as the Coles 316, support bridges like the Bailey Bridge System, Medium Girder Bridges, mines, explosives, road material such as Class 30 or 60 trackways, construction stores, and heavy plant like Terex tractors or caterpillars.

During battle the squadron's troops are usually spread out over the brigade's combat area, each field troop normally being attached to a battle group, squadron HQ colocated with brigade HQ, and echelon elements and resource troops staying in the holding area at the Forward Operating Base. The brigade commander, the artillery CO and the engineer squadron CO together form the Brigade TAC Group.

In the airmobile role the unit may have the task of laying bar mines from Chinooks; this can be of tactical advantage, but has the drawback of tying up important helicopter transport capacity for some time, and is not often done.

(Right) After bridging equipment is delivered to the crossing point down the brigade's chain of supply, it is the RE Field Troop's task to build the bridge. Here a double storey MGB (Medium Girder Bridge) is nearly completed, and pairs of sappers move the deck units into place. MGBs can be built in single and double storey configurations and with reinforcement piers. As an example, a 31m long double storey MGB can be constructed by a Field Troop in about 45 minutes, and can support vehicles up to Class 70. The material for this bridge would consist of ten pallets, each with a weight of 4 tons, which could be lifted to the bridging point in Chinooks.

(Below) The four combat engineer tractors of 51 Sqn are the only tracked vehicles in 24 Airmobile. Here one of the CETs moves across the newlybuilt MGB to check its load bearing capacity. The wide variety of tasks for the amphibious CET includes clearing obstacles, digging pits, preparing barriers and dragging vehicles out of difficult terrain. A rocket anchor linked to a 100m cable can be fired from the CET. The combat weight of the vehicle is 18.4 tons, and a 6-cylinder diesel gives it a speed of 52km/h (32mph).

An Ultralight Wheeled Tractor is lifted by an RAF Chinook HC2. The ULWT is a 4x4 digger-loader with front-mounted multipurpose bucket, used by the brigade engineers to dig trenches and ditches. Note the airportable harness; the first of the red ties preventing the cables from twisting has already pulled open. When the load is fully airborne all will be open and the harness will be spread without twisting. A twisted harness can lead to a spinning load, which in the worst cases can mean a helicopter going out of control. In suchcircumstances the crew – if they have enough altitude and time – are forced to dump the load to save the aircraft.

(**Left**) One of the main tasks of 51 Fd Sqn is mine clearing. Here a path through a minefield is cleared so that the infantry can advance. Equipped with a probe the first man of the clearance party (nicknamed the "ghost man") works his way forward, checking with a thin, flexible wire for any trip wires and then probing every few centimetres for suspicious objects in the ground. Note the angle at which the probe is used, to minimize pressure on the mine, whose detonation device is usually on the top surface; and the anti-fragmentation visor on his helmet.

(**Below**) The ghost man is normally followed by a second sapper who uses a probe to check the deeper levels. Behind this pair follows the mine detector man; here he is using an L77A1 device, with which he can locate the metallic content of a mine up to a depth of 0.7m (2ft 4ins) by pulse induction technology. Once a mine is found it is dug out and either disarmed, moved away, or marked and blown up later.

45

21 (Gibraltar 1779-1783) Air Defence Battery, Royal Artillery

Because of the threat to ground troops and helicopters on the modern battlefield from enemy fighter/ground attack aircraft and combat helicopters, the brigade needs its own integral, airportable air defence unit. 21 (Gibraltar 1779-1783) Air Defence Battery RA is part of 47 Regt RA, which supports 3rd (UK) Division; the regiment's other units are 10 (Assaye) Bty, supporting 1 Mech Bde from Tidworth, and 43 (Lloyd's Company) Bty, supporting 19 Inf Bde from Catterick. 21 Bty is based at Thorney Island. With six officers and 200 other ranks, it isstructured in three Air Defence Troops (D, E and F Troops), a Support Troop and a Battery HQ. Each of the troops breaks down into three sections each with four detachments, each with one Javelin SAM firing post; altogether the unit can field 36 Javelins. Javelin can be launched from the shoulder or, with multi-engagement capacity, from a Lightweight Multiple Launcher (LML). For the LML role three standard Javelin canisters and the standard shoulder launcher are clipped together with a tripod, a support tube and the LML head. Javelin is designed as a short range shoulder launched close air defence guided weapon system, with an effective range of 5500m (6,000 yards) against helicopters and 4500m (4,900 yards) against fast jets, an altitude up to 3000m (9,840 feet).

In the British Army Javelin replaced Blowpipe, being more sophisticated, with a greater range and a night sight; but at the time of writing Javelin itself is due to be replaced by the Starstreak High Velocity Missile (HVM), which can easily be retrofitted to the existing Javelin equipment. 21 Battery's firing posts are carried by Land Rover 110 with trailer, one per detachment, and the troop command elements are equipped with a Saxon command post vehicle. Altogether the unit's vehicle park consists of three Saxons, four 4-ton trucks, 50 B-type vehicles including Land Rovers, some of them FFR, and 43 trailers.

On operations the unit deploys its AD troops to key locations in the brigade area, e.g. Brigade Main, Forward Operating Base, artillery fire bases or helicopter landing sites, as well as along specific routes to cover moves by ground forces or helicopter operations. If brigade units are operating behind enemy lines air defence detachments are deployed along with them by helicopter, and provide lethal close air protection.

Together with the unit's Javelin and Starstreak HVM the Air Defence Alerting Device is deployed. ADAD operates as an infrared search and tracking system against fast, low-flying aircraft including both jets and combat helicopters, and supports the firing detachments by early identification of the threat. This passive system, made by Thorn EMI, is all-weather day and night capable; it can store up to four targets in priority order and direct the launcher operator to the right target, thus speeding up the process of engagement.

(Left) Their Land Rover and trailer have been dropped by the Chinook in the background, and these gunners of 21 AD Bty have left the helicopter to stow their kit in the vehicle. Shortly they will move out to establish their Javelin LML on a perimeter around a key bridge on the MND(C) main supply route during an exercise in Denmark.

(Above) Leaving the helicopter landing site, these soldiers carry Javelin SAMs in containers; the shoulder-held launchers are packed in their Bergens. Soon they will spread out around the location to provide an air defence screen for further incoming helicopter loads. Normally the launchers are deployed forward of the vital points (HLS, FOB, FARP, etc.) in order to provide ideal cover. Especially when the brigade is operating well ahead of the FLOT enemy air attack is a major threat to airportable assets, and elements of 21 AD Bty are always part of the first wave to be flown in.

(Above right) The Air Defence Alerting Device is used by 21 AD Bty to support firing detachments by identifying the relative threat of low-flying enemy aircraft sooner, so that the alerted detachment can engage the attacking aircraft earlier and in order of urgency, which gives a higher efficiency.

(Above) The ADAD is usually placed near the LML, and the operator is linked via field telephone to the firing team. The radar is mounted on a tripod and the operator uses a hand-held control panel.

(Right) Javelin LML deployed in a trench along a helicopter flying corridor. Javelin employs semi-automatic command to line of sight guidance (SACLOS), and its range of 4500m against fast-moving aircraft enables it to neutralize them before they can release their weapons. The LML consists of three standard Javelin canistered missiles and a shoulder launcher which are clipped together onto a support tube with a tripod and the LML head.

(Below) A Javelin SAM just leaving an LML. The rocket weighs 12.7kg (28lbs); the field handling canister together with the missile weighs 19kg (41lbs). Inside the missile is a 2.74kg (6lb) HE fragmentation warhead detonated by either contact or a proximity fuse.

19 Airmobile Field Ambulance, Royal Army Medical Corps

Because the brigade may mount offensive operations behind the enemy front line, the specially designed 19 Airmobile Field Ambulance RAMC, based at Colchester, provides second line casualty evacuation and medical support; with a war strength of 41 officers and 241 other ranks, it consists of an HQ, a Rear Squadron and a Forward Squadron. In the front line five Medical Sections, each with a doctor and ten medics, support and assist the battle groups' regimental first aid posts (RAPs). Here the casualty's situation is improved and he is prepared for evacuation. The aim of the Medical Sections and RAPs is to ensure that every casualty is seen by a doctor not more than one hour after his injury; care during this so-called "golden hour" has been proved statistically to give even the most seriously wounded higher rates of survival.

Each of the five sections is equipped with two Land Rovers with trailers, one of them FFR. Together with the HQ element, and a psychiatric section of two doctors and three medics, they form the Collecting Troop, one half of the Forward Squadron. The other half is the Ambulance Troop with its 1-ton Land Rover ambulances; these will soon be replaced by the new Land Rover 130 ambulance. The 49 NCOs and soldiers commanded by one officer pick up the casualties at the medical section locations and transport them to the Airmobile Dressing Station (ADS). Depending on the brigade's tasks and the battle scenario this may be done by helicopter.

The ADS can operate either as one complete facility or be split into a Light and a Heavy Airmobile Dressing Station (LADS and HADS). The LADS can be flown forward in one lift by a Chinook and a Lynx if the battle situation allows it. Usually this is done if casualty evacuation from the front line turns out to be complicated or has to cover long distances. Ideally the LADS and HADS should be positioned in buildings, but they can also be established in the field with large tents.

Once established, the LADS with its 18-25 personnel has the equipment and skills to treat up to 200 casualties with all types of wounds, and to provide second line support for up to 24 hours. Here the casualties are given basic treatment and are either returned to their unit or, in more serious cases, are sent further back. As equipment is limited, the LADS normally comprises the tents and medical instruments and supplies together with one ATMP for moving equipment and personnel from the landing site.

If necessary the HADS can also be flown to forward locations by two Chinooks with internal and underslung loads, to link up with the LADS; but it is often found with the Brigade Support Group. While the LADS, with its three treatment bays, essentially comprises the reception part of the dressing station, the HADS comprises the treatment element, with five treatment bays and two surgical teams, and the evacuation element, with two more treatment bays. The complete ADS can deal with 450 casualties in 24 hours. The two Forward Surgical Teams (FST) of the unit, one of them attached from the TA, can perform a variety of live-saving operations as well as amputations, arresting internal bleeding and treating fractures. For further treatment the casualty

is evacuated to third line medical support, normally being collected by a field hospital's own Ambulance Support Group. If necessary the FST can be deployed forward with the LADS so that a casualty is treated surgically within six hours wherever possible.

History shows that many soldiers in wartime are lost to disease rather than enemy action. To prevent diseases an environmental health team of specially trained soldiers, also known as the Hygiene Team, can be formed to assist unit commanders and train the brigade's soldiers in preventative precautions. The Gulf War showed that a significant number of casualties in the build-up phase of operations have been dental casualties. Even these can be treated by 19 AFA, which has a fully

Most of a Light Airmobile Dressing Station is visible in this one photo. The underslung net which this Chinook HC2 is lifting from the back of a 4-ton Bedford truck contains all tentage, equipment, stretchers, medical and surgical supplies and instruments which the LADS crew will need to get into action in the forward area. As inside load the Chinook is carrying a Supercat Mk.2 ATMP and some of the medical personnel; the rest of the team, which can be up to 25 strong, will be flown in by a Lynx Mk.9.

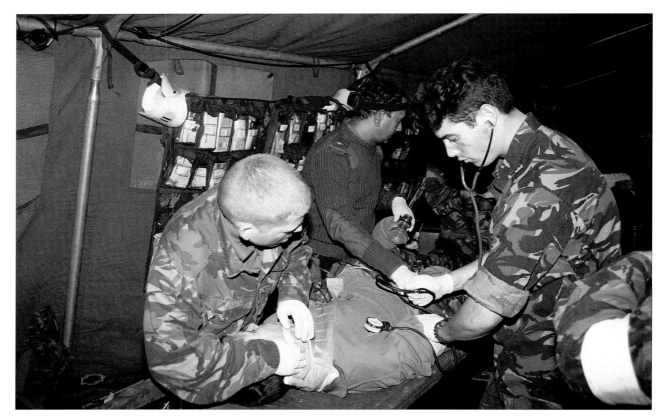

(**Above**) One of the three treatment bays of the LADS, manned by a doctor and two medical orderlies; they are stabilizing the condition of a simulated casualty. Note, strapped unfolded to the tent harness, their special medical packs.

(**Right**) A medic poses with his special version of the PLCE rucksack, packed with everything necessary for the initial stabilization of casualties. Note his red cross patch, MND(C) patch and brigade patch; and the hypodermics, transfusion bottle, dressings, bandages, ointments and medical instruments in the rucksack.

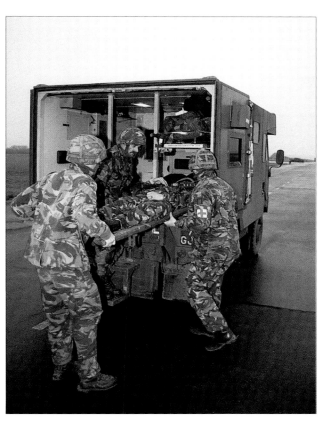

(Above) After a helicopter with casualties from the battlefield arrives in the FOB the wounded are carried to the HADS by ambulance. The 1-ton Land Rover ambulance can carry up to four stretcher cases.

(Above right) In the head registration compartment a medic checks the documents of a casualty who has just arrived for further treatment. Here the patient's details are taken, and he is then moved to an empty treatment bay. Because paperwork can get misplaced, the most vital information about the treatment already given – e.g., morphine injections – is also written on the casualty's forehead. When a casualty arrives at the HADS he has seen at least one doctor already, who has given lifesaving first aid so that he could be evacuated to the brigade rear area. In the HADS all necessary treatment will be carried out to stabilize his condition for further evacuation to the field hospital.

(Right) For the medics and doctors of 19 AFA every exercise brings both the treatment of simulated casualties (or highly realistic medical dummies, for more serious wounds); and the real job of treating all kinds of injuries which result from the inevitable accidents during training. Instruction in front line medical skills is to an extremely high level, and medics are accustomed to reacting to emergencies at a few seconds' notice.

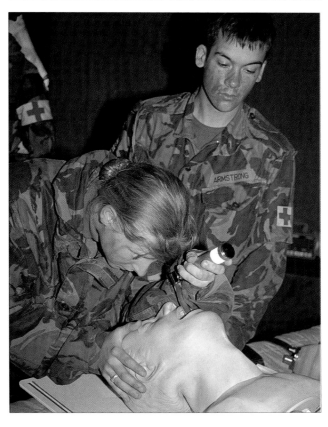

equipped dental team. For incidents like traffic accidents a so-called "trauma team" can be formed to move forward by helicopter; they can either land or abseil down to deal with casualties on the spot and prepare them for evacuation to the ADS.

The Rear Squadron comprises an HQ element and a Support Troop which provides fuel, rations and medical supplies to the unit. The Field Ambulance has 25 Land Rovers with trailer, 18 x 1-ton ambulances, 16 x 4-ton DAF trucks with trailer (one of them a fuel tanker), four ATMPs and two motorcycles.

24 Airmobile Brigade Provost Unit

The Brigade Provost Unit (BPU), Royal Military Police is based at Colchester where it forms part of 156 Provost Company, RMP. The BPU consists of two officers and 66 soldiers, organized in an HQ element and two platoons.

During operations the main tasks of the unit are route reconnaissance, traffic control and convoy escort. Within Brigade HQ the RMP desk monitors the movement of all convoys and keeps track of where they are located at all times. This is necessary in case of redirection, e.g. if a bridge is blown, or if enemy forces cut one of the brigade's Main Supply Routes (MSR) the brigade commander can be immediately informed as to which elements have already passed the trouble spots. The convoys are given routes, timings, speeds, starting times and possible break points. At the start point the RMP check the time and number of vehicles against their convoy report and release the vehicles appropriately. The convoy then follows the signposted route, passing through RMP Traffic Posts (TP) until it reaches the release point. At each TP the vehicles are again counted. To establish the TPs the unit has 20 Land Rovers FFR and 13 motorcycles for tactical work, as well as some civilian vehicles for garrison use.

The civil side of the RMP's work often involves liaison with civil police and MOD police. A number of soldiers of 156 Provost Coy are members of the RMP Special Investigation

(Above) Member of 156 Provost Coy, RMP, patrolling near an important bridge on one of the brigade's Main Supply Routes. Armed with his L85A1, he clearly displays all the RMP's field recognition features: bright scarlet beret with RMP badge, MP sleeve patch and "visibility vest".

(Left) A supply convoy of Foden 8x4 Low Mobility Tankers is waved through an RMP traffic post, where the number of vehicles and their timings are noted so that the convoy has a controlled journey and MSRs are not blocked by traffic jams or breakdowns. The LMT carries 22,500 litres in five compartments and weighs 29-tons loaded; powered by a Rolls Royce 6-cylinder diesel, it can reach a top speed of 76km/h (47mph).

Branch, which deals with criminal offences in which military personnel are involved. Their work includes preserving evidence at the scene of a crime, checking the particulars of those involved and searching for suspects. The unit provides an investigation element to 24 Airmobile Brigade HQ for investigating serious crimes within the brigade.

The brigade commander is supported by the RMP in maintaining military discipline and enforcing the law, in the handling of prisoners of war and escorting senior personnel. They also advise brigade units on security, prevent crime, and warn soldiers of specific risks to their lives. In airmobile operations the BPU can provide a Fly Forward Section to the battle groups, including one Land Rover and four motorcycles with six men who are able to provide the fighting elements with all the main combat support tasks normally carried out by the RMP.

(Below) At the start point for a convoy in the FOB, an RMP team at work from a Land Rover FFR with two motorbike despatch riders attached. Signposting of MSRs and circuits in the FOB and staging area is done by the RMP with small black plates bearing directions or symbols (e.g. an axe, a gryphon, etc.) together with arrows – see foreground; drivers identify their route by the symbols and the direction by the arrow.

(Right) This Harley Davidson has replaced the VB 1010 Armstrong MT500 in a variety of liaison and traffic control tasks with brigade units including the BPU; its 350cc engine gives a top speed of 128kp/h (80mph) and a range of 139km (87 miles). The weight of 366kg (740lbs) includes two document panniers and a carrier for the L85A1 rifle.

Brigade Combat Service & Support Battalion

Logistic and equipment support for 24 Airmobile Brigade is provided by the Colchester-based CSS Bn, comprising 15 Logistic Sqn, 4 Airmobile Support Sqn, 8 Field Workshop REME, and the battalion HQ. In peacetime the battalion fields 337 officers and men, and in wartime the strength increases to 456 personnel. During operations 72 Aircraft Workshop, which is part of 7 Bn REME based at Wattisham, is cross-attached under command of the CSS Battalion.

On operations the CSS Bn establishes and controls the supply chain which transports the logistics forward. The chain begins at the Theatre Holding Area (THA), which is normally established and operated by corps or division troops. If the brigade operates under, e.g., MND(C) command, a British CSS Group with additional support groups from Germany, the Netherlands and Belgium sets up the THA. Here the 24 Airmobile Bde CSS Bn picks up the necessary stores and moves them to the Brigade Staging Area, which can be several hundred miles from the THA. For this task the battalion is supported by an additional logistic squadron from the TA or the Regular Army, e.g. 28 Gurkha Transport Squadron of 10 Transport Regiment; the unit fulfilled this role on exercise "Gryphon's Eye 97".

The logistical side of the Brigade Staging Area is established by 4 Airmobile Support Sqn, and is termed Brigade Support Group (Rear). It consists of at least two storage areas though the number can range up to five. Each storage area holds all types of stores, divided between the separate areas to prevent stores of any one kind being destroyed in a single enemy bombardment. Altogether the storage areas can occupy up to seven square kilometers (2.7sq/m). The range of possible stored supplies at BSG(R) includes ammunition, rations, clothing and spare parts, up to equipment like concertina wire, sand bags, trackways, Medium Girder Bridges and other heavy engineer material – every type of supplied item except for water, which is the responsibility of the Royal Engineers.

One of the storage areas also accomodates a Bulk Fuel Installation where aviation fuel and diesel is stored in 136 and 45 cubic meter rubber tanks, which are normally dug into the ground. Altogether the unit can hold up to 250,000 litres in the BFI and another 110,000 litres in tankers (55,000 and 24,200 gallons). The CSS Bn HQ is also located at BSG(R) and is linked with an additional smaller HQ at BSG (Forward); both command and control elements are established by the HQ squadron, which also provides the necessary communications and administrative support for the unit.

BSG (Forward) is operated by 15 Logistic Sqn and is normally situated beween the battalions' areas of responsibility and BSG(R). BSG(F) is a smaller version of BSG(R), normally situated in about one square kilometer (0.38 sq/m) of woodland; it consists of all equipment needed for the battlegroups, to allow freedom of action and keep the chain of supply short. From BSG(F) stores are moved forward to distribution points which are dispersed for tactical reasons. Here they are collected by the

units; it is also possible for 15 Logistic Sqn to supply equipment and stores directly to the units, but this is only done if the operational situation does not allow a unit to collect them. If the operational situation does not demand distribution points, units may pick their stores up directly from BSG (Forward).

So how does the CSS Bn know what is needed and where? Twice every day a Logistic Situation Report (LogSitRep) is completed by every unit, which includes what they hold and what they will require in the next 12 hours. When the LogSitRep reaches the CSS Bn HQ it is passed to 4 Airmobile Support Sqn where the stores are collected, put together on the "flat-racks" of the DROPS (Demountable Rack Off-loading & Pick-up System), and moved forward to the BFG(F) or the distribution point.

For urgent requests, or when an airmobile battlegroup is operating behind the Forward Line of Enemy Troops (FLET), the CSS Bn runs the Logistic Helicopter Landing Site. By sending a HelQuest to the Brigade HQ Air Cell the unit anounces its need of helicopter transport capacity. The Air Cell issues a HelTask, which will go to the CSS Bn as well as to the helicopter unit with all necessary orders. The aircraft will pick up the material prepared for airlift and deliver it to the unit. Even fuel can be delivered by the use of Air Portable Fuel Carriers (APFC).

While each unit of the brigade deploys with all necessary stores to fight a battle lasting up to two days, the CSS Bn holds stores for another three days, and is backed by the Theatre Holding Area with stores for an additional 25 days. For example: the stored ammunition for three days for all units of 24 Airmobile Bde, from 5.56mm rounds to 105mm shells, hand grenades, Milan anti-tank rockets, mortar bombs, engineer mines, etc., has a total weight of 440 tons.

The Royal Electrical & Mechanical Engineers' 8 Field Workshop is the third component of the CSS Bn, providing first

A logistic revolution took place when the Demountable Rack Off-load & Pick-up System (DROPS) was introduced by the British Army in 1990. Using pallets or "flat-racks" capable of carrying loads of up to 15 tons, DROPS vehicles equipped with their own integral lifting system can load and unload quickly and without external help; so the same vehicle can transport more loads within a shorter time. The CSS Bn is equipped with the Medium Mobility Load Carrier (MMLC) produced by Leyland; artillery units fielding AS90 and MLRS use the Improved model (IMMLC) built by Foden due to its higher cross-country capabilities. Both are 8x6 trucks and use the Multilift Mk.4 loading system.

(Opposite bottom) Two DROPS trucks destined for the FOB, loading up with the pallets onto which all standard ammunition and other ordnance stores can be packed.

(Below) A column of DROPS vehicles from 28 Gurkha Transport Sqn – note the red crossed kukris painted below the driver's windscreen – transferring ammunition from the Theatre Staging Area to the Brigade Staging Area. The Leyland 8x6 DROPS trucks have a crew of two and weigh 32 tons fully loaded; they can also tow a trailer with an additional maximum weight of 20 tons. Powered by a Perkins 6-cylinder turbo-charged diesel, they have a top speed of 75km/h (46mph) and a road range of 500km (310 miles).

The JCB 410M 4x4 forklift can move NATO pallets of up to 1,815kg (3,993lbs) weight over rough terrain. The low profile JCB weighs 6,850kg (15,070lbs) and can easily be airlifted. This is a Royal Logistic Corps JCB 410M of the brigade CSS Bn loading DROPS flat-racks with its forklift, but buckets, sweepers or crane hooks can be fitted instead; the vehicle is also in use with the Royal Engineers.

line repair support to battalion vehicles as well as second line repair support to all vehicles of the brigade. The Field Workshop works closely with the REME Light Aid Detachments (LADs) of the brigade units. Broken down vehicles and damaged equipment are assessed by the unit LADs; normally every repair which would take them longer than two hours is passed over to the Forward Repair Group (FRG) of 8 Field Workshop. The FRG is located as close as possible to the Forward Line of Own Troops, and carries out all immediate repairs which can be completed in up to ten hours. While the FRG mainly exchanges parts like engines, gearboxes, water pumps, etc., the skills of the REME personnel include welding, forging and electrical repairs.

Attached to the FRG is a Forward Repair Team (FRT) which supports the LAD in the repair and maintenance of optronics, radios, computers, night vision equipment, laser rangefinders and other electrical or electronic equipment. With their two Land Rovers and one ATMP (All Terrain Mobile Platform) the FRT can work in the battlegroups' operational areas, and carry all necessary tools to check and adjust equipment as well as changing defective parts. If it is possible, the FRG and MRG (Main Repair Group) together with the HQ of 8 Field Workshop are established within buildings where hard standing is available. This makes life easier for the mechanics, but every task can equally be carried out in the field if need be. If the FRG cannot fix a defect it is forwarded with a report to the MRG, where almost every imaginable repair can be carried out even if the REME soldiers have to build their own spare parts on a lathe.

15 Logistic Squadron Heavy Equipment
22 x DROPS
 5 x 22500l tankers
 3 x 12000l tankers
 6 x 4500l Bedford tankers
 8 x 8-ton trucks
19 x trailers
 8 x Land Rovers (GS & FFR)
 1 Foden recovery vehicle

4 Airmobile Support Sqn Heavy Equipment
11 x DROPS
11 x 14-ton trucks
 9 x 4-ton trucks
27 x trailers
 7 x GCB tractors
18 x Land Rovers

8 Field Workshop REME Heavy Equipment
10 x 4-ton trucks with container workshops
18 x 4-ton trucks
 3 x 14-ton trucks
14 x trailers
 6 x Foden recovery vehicles
14 x Land Rovers

When on operations the DROPS fleet may be increased from 33 to up to 80 vehicles.

Anything which turns out to be unrepairable is sent to the Equipment Collection Point for return to depots, where it is either written off or given a total overhaul.

In its ten container workshops on 4-ton trucks, the MRG also has the capability to check, adjust and repair every piece of equipment that cannot be fixed in the field by the FRT. Especially for the repair of highly sophisticated equipment like Milan missile launchers, CWS night vision equipment or Clansman PRC range radios a dry room is needed, and for this the container workshops are ideal.

Whereas 8 Field Workshop deals with all type of ground forces equipment, the soldiers of 72 Aircraft Workshop do all aircraft maintenance which cannot be carried out by the AAC regiments' own workshops. This 160-strong unit fields 65 vehicles ranging from Land Rovers and trailers up to 14-ton trucks, and is subdivided into an HQ & Support Platoon, two Close Support Platoons, a General Support Platoon and an Aircraft Support Group. While first line basic flying maintenance is carried out at unit level, the second line maintenance provided by 72 Aircraft Workshop means that given a suitable location in the Brigade Operational Area it can strip down a complete aircraft. Dealing with the Lynxes and Gazelles of the Army Air Corps, the REME's skills include difficult jobs like changing gearboxes, rotorheads and engines. The tasks of 72 Workshop are divided between the Close Support Platoons, which undertake all the work on complete aircraft, and the General Support Platoon, who work on specific components, divided between avionics and mechanical parts. The Aircraft Support Group holds all necessary spares – more than 2,500 items, from rotorheads to nuts and bolts, and including all the spares for the unit's special electronic testing equipment.

A section from 51 Fd Sqn RE is attached to the CSS Bn to build up a security perimeter for the storage sites, level ground, establish power lines, prepare roads and dig slopes for the BFI, as well as performing any other necessary engineering tasks. They also look after the stored engineer equipment, and make sure that necessary engineer stores are prepared for their squadron's Field Troops.

Although they normally operate out of sight of the combat troops, the soldiers of the CSS Bn are one of the key elements in a successful operation; every soldier should remember that without their back-up no battle could ever be won.

(**Right, top**) REME craftsman of 72 Aircraft Workshop working on the rotorhead of a Gazelle. If they can set up in a suitable location the REME unit can carry out the complete range of second line maintenance including the B5 inspection, which involves a nearly complete stripdown of the aircraft while all parts are checked.

(**Right, centre**) A mechanic of the Main Repair Group repairs the front brakes on a Land Rover 109. 8 Fd Workshop REME can maintain and repair every piece of brigade equipment from DROPS trucks to assault rifles and from binoculars to radios.

(**Right**) MRG mechanic welding up damage to the body of a Bedford truck. A wide range of skills are available among the REME personnel, including telecommunication technicians, blacksmiths, vehicle mechanics and electricians, recovery mechanics, etc.

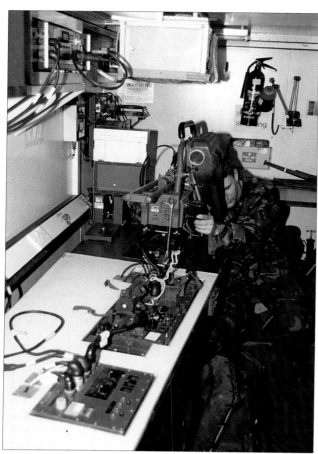

(**Left**) Inside the MRG's ten workshop containers based on 4-ton trucks all the necessary resources are available to test and repair highly sophisticated equipment. Although photographed here in a container this equipment for checking the Milan ATGW sighting and tracking system is normally deployed as far forward as possible with the infantry, and operated by soldiers of the FRT. Because of their hard use under war conditions weapon systems like Milan require regular inspection and maintenance.

(**Below**) Soldiers of the CSS Bn prepare a Bedford 4x4 4500-litre tanker to be refuelled from a Bulk Fuel Installation at BSG (Forward). With their tankers and the fuel stored in the BFI, the CSS Bn reserve totals around 360,000 litres (nearly 80,000 gallons).

(Left) Bulk Fuel Installations are dug into the ground to hold 24 Airmobile Bde's fuel resupplies. The large flat rubber tanks come in 136 and 45 cubic meter sizes. BFIs for diesel and aviation fuel are usually established at BSG (Rear) and BSG (Forward). Here a soldier of the CSS Bn checks a link while fuel is pumped from a Foden tanker into the BFI.

(Below) Filled with 1892 litres of fuel each, Airportable Fuel Carriers are lined up along a runway on an abandoned airfield which was used as FOB during a brigade exercise. During combat operations APFCs are brought into the field as underslung loads together with Forward Area Refuelling Equipment, which consists of petrol engine driven centrifugal pumps, closed circuit refuelling nozzles and pipes, valves and fittings.

Multinational Division Central (Airmobile)

The Multinational Division Central (Airmobile) – MND(C) – was one of the first activated of the newly structured NATO forces designed for flexible deployment in a variety of missions including conventional high level combat scenarios, crisis management, peacekeeping, disaster relief and humanitarian aid.

The formation was first raised in an *ad hoc* move for an experimental exercise called "Certain Shield 91"; at that date it was termed Multinational Airmobile Division (MNAD). On 15 January 1992 Belgium, Germany, the Netherlands and the United Kingdom signed a memorandum of understanding covering the establishment and operation of an activation staff for a multinational headquarters to command and control MND(C). HQ MND(C) started work in April 1992, and the division was fully activated in April 1994. 24 Airmobile Bde provides one quarter of the division's combat forces, together with the German 31. Luftlandebrigade (31 Airborne Brigade), the Belgian Brigade Para-Commando, and the Dutch 11 Luchtmobiele Brigade.

31.Luftlandebrigade consists of two airborne infantry battalions, each with 12 x Milan; one airborne anti tank battalion with 36 x Wiesel weapons carriers with TOW and 24 x Wiesels with 20mm cannon; one airborne mortar company with 12 x 120mm mortars; a brigade HQ and signal company, an engineer company and a combat service and support company.

The Belgian *Brigade Para-Commando* fields two airborne infantry battalions each with six x 81mm mortars and 18 x Milan; a reconnaissance battalion with 48 x Iltis equipped with .50cal machine guns, 12 of them mounting Milan; an artillery battery with 12 x 105mm howitzers; an air defence battery with 18 x Mistral SAM systems; an engineer company with plant, mine-laying and mine-clearing equipment; a field ambulance company, a large logistic company and an HQ company.

The Dutch *11 Luchtmobiele Brigade* has three airmobile infantry battalions each with 12 x TOW and 9 x Dragon ATGW systems, 9 x 81mm mortars and 18 x Stinger air defence systems; a combat engineer company, a medical company, a maintenance and repair company and a supply and transport company. Attached to the brigade is the Royal Netherlands Air Force Tactical Helicopter Group, with CH47D Chinook and Cougar transport helicopters (the latter being similar to the British Puma, and Apache AH64A and AH64D combat helicopters.

For 1998 it is planned that the division should be able to field 85 transport helicopters (Puma, Cougar, CH47 Chinook and CH53); 38 anti-tank helicopters (A109, Lynx TOW, and BO105 PAH – equivalent to the Lynx Mk.7, with six HOT anti-tank missiles); 12 attack helicopters (AH64 Apache); and 73 observation, reconnaissance and LBH helicopters (A109, Lynx, Gazelle and BO105 UBH). This total of 208 helicopters is planned to increase to 232 in the year 2000 when all 30 Apaches of the RNAF batch are in service.

Including its combat support and combat service support units, the division has a strength of up to 20,000 soldiers. Equipment and training are focused on rapid inter-regional deployment. The MND(C) sends a strong signal of alliance

(Above) During the MND(C) exercise "Cold Grouse 95" this camouflaged ADA gunner of 21 (Gibraltar) Bty RA provides close protection to one of the battery's Javelin detachments. Note the Union flag and MND(C) patch on his left sleeve. He is armed with an L85A1 rifle with "iron sights", standard for all non-infantry units.

(Opposite, top) Every year one of the four brigades under MND(C) command organizes a brigade-size exercise in which elements of the other brigades take part. Cross-training is carried out to familiarize soldiers of the different national units under command with their allies' equipment and standard operating procedures. Here a Gurkha from B Coy, 1st Royal Scots fires a 7.62mm German MG3 under instruction by a German paratrooper from 314. Fallschirmjägerbataillon during exercise "Artful Issue 97" at Sennelager in Germany.

(Opposite, bottom) The MND(C) transport fleet of 85 aircraft includes a couple of German Heeresflieger CH53G helicopters, each of which has a total internal/underslung payload of 8000kg (17,600lbs). It can accomodate 37 fully equipped troops, 23 stretcher cases, or two of these "Wiesel" light armoured weapons carriers. This Wiesel of 272. Fallschirmpanzer-abwehrbataillon (airborne anti-tank battalion) is armed with a 20mm cannon, but the TOW anti-tank guided missile system can also be fitted. During MND(C) operations Wiesels often operate together with the reconnaissance elements of 24 Airmobile Brigade, providing a recce screen or slowing down an enemy advance.

capabilities and resolve, and it should defuse tension by providing a highly visible and capable deterrence force. On operations the MND(C) is under command of ARRC (Allied Rapid Reaction Corps), which is the land component of the newly formed NATO rapid reaction forces. The division provides a key element in reinforcing reaction forces; it is prepared to fight alongside them, or on its own, if crisis management has failed. The Brigade Para-Commando (BE) and 31. Luftlandebrigade (GE) are airborne trained, while 11 Luchtmobiele Brigade (NL) and 24 Airmobile Brigade (UK) are airmobile infantry brigades with helicopter assets.

In addition to the divisional HQ and the four national brigades, a full range of divisional troops is assigned to MND(C) to give the division operational capabilities for all the tasks expected of a formation of this kind. The divisional and combat support units include a Belgian ground reconnaissance battalion, a Dutch artillery battalion, a British air-defence battalion, a German observation and recce helicopter company, a German anti-NBC company, a British artillery observation post battery as well as an electronic warfare unit and a long range artillery surveillance, recce and target acquisition unit.

On the CSS side, Germany attaches a transport battalion and a transport helicopter unit; and Germany, the Netherlands and Belgium contribute a National Support Group which provides hospital, maintenance, supply and transport elements to their respective national elements of the division. For the UK this is done by elements of the Combat Service & Support Group. To be fully operational the division requires two additional support battalions and a military police unit, which are drawn from other force structures as well as host nation support. A Dutch signal battalion and a German HQ company provide direct support to the divisional HQ staff.

Today the MND(C) is one of the leading examples of multinational co-operation and interoperability within the new NATO defence concept, and 24 Airmobile Brigade forms an important part of it.

(Above) 301 Sqn, RNAF are the first unit attached to MND(C) using the Apache AH64A attack helicopter. Currently 12 Apaches leased from the USA are operational; these are due to be replaced by AH64D Apache Longbow in 1998, and the complete batch of 30 will be operational by 2002. With a top speed of 270km/h (167mph) and a range of 460-485km (285-300 miles) or 2.5 flying hours, the Apache can carry up to 16 Hellfire guided rockets, or 76 multi purpose 2.75in rockets, or 4 Stinger anti-aircraft missiles, or a mix of all of them, plus its 30mm cannon with sights slaved to the pilot's helmet. The main RNAF transport machine is the AS 532 Cougar MKH, of which 300 Sqn fields 17; they have a lift capacity of 4.5 tons internal/underslung and can accomodate 16 troops and their kit.

(Opposite, top) Dropped by an RAF Chinook HC2, a German section from 5 Kompanie, 314. Fallschirmjägerbataillon spread out in a half circle to the front of the helicopter to provide protection while the aircraft is on the ground. With the exception of the Chinook with its rear ramp, deploying troops usually leave helicopters through side doors and head forward left and right,

so that the pilot can see them. Special care is taken not to enter the rear left quarter – the danger zone of the tail rotor.

Later during exercise "Gryphon's Eye 94" the German paratroopers evacuated "threatened villagers" from Cophill Down on Salisbury Plain. Because of NATO's strong involvement in peace keeping and peace enforcing operations this type of scenario is now an integral part of the annual MND(C) exercises.

(Opposite, bottom left) Among the British units assigned to MND(C) is an element of the Honourable Artillery Company (the oldest unit in the British Army, which traces its lineage back to the 16th century). The HAC's task today is to provide artillery OPs and general reconnaissance deep behind enemy lines. As with the SAS, an HAC patrol is usually four strong and can operate independently for several days. Equipment typically includes Spyglass, a hand held thermal imaging observation aid; GPS; laser rangefinders; and PRC 319 HF/VHF radio. For the camara this OP was "discamouflaged"; on operations it is nearly impossible to spot them.

(**Bottom right**) One of the scenarios for which MND(C) trains most intensively is working on the borders between the different brigades' areas of responsibility. If the enemy attacks here it is important that two or more nationalities are able to operate together, and manoeuvre around another brigade location. Here Belgian Para-Commandos armed with FNC assault rifles operate under command of the German 31 Airborne Bde, some of whose paratroopers are seen in the background.

(**Overleaf**) A Chinook lifts a Land Rover and trailer; the HLS for this load will be the artillery fire base, which will become the next FOB as the battle progresses.